Dundee

Edited by
James Barrowman

Dostoyevsky Wannabe Cities

An Imprint of Dostoyevsky Wannabe

First Published in 2019
by Dostoyevsky Wannabe Cities
All rights reserved
© All copyright reverts to individual authors

Dostoyevsky Wannabe Cities is an imprint of
Dostoyevsky Wannabe publishing.

www.dostoyevskywannabe.com

Cover design by Dostoyevsky Wannabe

ISBN-9781093890068

Dostoyevsky Wannabe Cities books represent a snapshot of the
writing of a particular locale at a particular moment in time. The
content is reflective of the choices of the guest-editor.

Dedicated to Jim Stewart

Contents

Preface

Many thanks to Dostoyevsky Wannabe, for allowing us the opportunity to share the range and diversity of writing currently coming out of Dundee. From new writers still at the university and gaining their first publication, to experienced and accomplished scrievers that are keen to advocate for their city – all sorts of writers, and writing styles, are represented in this anthology.

I would also like to thank my colleagues at Caffè Nero on the Murraygate, I have been permitted to use the coffeeshop after-hours as a venue for Amplify Dundee – a writing group founded on the principles of collaboration and independent publishing. This has allowed me to guest-edit this book in an open and encouraging manner, with a fortnightly forum where writers were able to ask questions about the book and workshop their pieces in front of the team. This has been a truly rewarding experience, and it has served to make the submissions process as accessible as possible.

James Barrowman

The Tenth Circle

'It is a pity that Dante could not be brought back and compelled to live in Dundee for a little; he would add a sensational new circle to his Inferno.'

Hugh MacDiarmid

If Dundee was to have a Modernist mascot, it would have to be one of the foremost literary flâneurs from Europe, because MacDiarmid and his disciples hated us too much: perhaps Baudelaire, for his frequent drug use, outstanding debts, and vicious criticism of everyone he held dear; Benjamin, due to his passion for decaying shopping malls, his acknowledgement of the mythic nature of 'progress', and the tragic irony of his death; or, my personal choice, Fernando Pessoa, given that today Dundee still stands firm as a monument to everything that is obscure, anonymous, and fragmentary. Dundee is disquietude, and this is what I think of as I cross the Tay Rail Bridge, forever haunted by the disaster that struck the previous structure, *to be remembered for a very long time.*

As we approach the train station, I lean back in exhaustion only to overhear an overloud conversation from the two boys seated behind me:

'Eh swear tae god man, one look and eh knew. Am on the dancefloor, not a care in the world, til a look across and meet her eyes. Shimmied ower, got her a drink, grabbed her number – before eh know it the club's shut and eh've lost sight ae her. Eh text her but naething yet.'

'Eh wes the same when eh met Jennifer mate – hit me like a bolt ae lightnin. When ye know, ye know.'

'Eh cannae stop thinking aboot her Drew! Am eh in love?'

At this point I tune out. I like to think I am a romantic of some sort, but I can't stand this sort of saccharine chat. I think that Dante has a lot to answer for. 'The Man Who Invented Sweethearts', like calling Cervantes 'The Man Who Invented Fiction', as if either of these things constitute a legitimate invention. Such is the degraded state of the arts in this country, that we must appropriate the language of science to justify the veneration we give to the world's greatest writers. At least Cervantes, when he imagined fiction, imagined something useful and necessary. Dante for all of his magnitude, imagined something truly damaging. Dante is a liar. Dante gave us the impression that love can be exchanged from just one look, that love is accessible to anybody that possesses a pair of eyes and a sense of entitlement – that love is not something that builds and grows, something that must be earned. Dante is the square root of a hundred Disney cartoons and romantic comedies. Dante is the origin story for a thousand incels, pick-up-artists and men's rights activists. Dante also perpetuated the distinction between romance and friendship – despite the fact he probably had many more loving moments with Cavalcanti than he ever did with Beatrice, and this young man likely has a stronger attachment to Drew than he does to Jennifer.

God, I'm touchy today – maybe a walk will do me good.

Dundee is the ideal location for the budding Scottish flâneur. A benefit of its status as a 'monstrously overgrown small town' is the short walking-distance from one end of the city to the next, alongside the accessibility of many characteristic towns and villages just beyond the city borders. Dundee's frenzy of architectural style also lends itself to a wandering mind – as the urban explorer strolls in a straight line through a medieval, Victorian, Art Deco, and futurist cityscape. Whole epochs lie juxtaposed on a single block, with the hideous and the sublime often contained within one crumbling tenement or abandoned shopfront. Dundee, *the gift of God*, is the Scottish centre of the dichotomy, modern Britain's carnivalesque capital. This is at its most apparent during a short walk through the city centre, especially in the Caird Hall vicinity – where one is stopped by the minute to be asked for various things from the full range of Dundee hawkers. These include but are not limited to the city's abundance of

Mormons and other Christian missionaries, charity workers, homeless people in desperate need, and the resurrected Dundee 'worthy', willing to sing a song or spin a tale in return for loose change or a spare cigarette.

As I emerge into the train station, a flimsy veneer of sheen barely conceals an empty space lacking the luxuries of a shop or public benches. I am painfully hungover, *hingin oot ma erse*, and my condition is accelerated by the use of the public piano in the station – where an elderly woman is effortlessly playing the first of Erik Satie's *Gymnopédies*. This is profoundly new, as usually the piano is reserved for the butchered performance of My Heart Will Go On, Greensleeves, or at the very best, Moonlight Sonata. Not long after its installation the piano was beaten up and destroyed by a group of youths (somehow placed beyond the boundaries of the security cameras), seemingly outraged by the mere suggestion that something as useless as a piano could be bestowed upon commuters as a 'gift'. The new, crowdfunded instrument is better protected, and I stand in a hypnotic trance as she conjures up a Parisian café. Satie, who MacDiarmid is keen to remind us had Scottish ancestry, wrote the most beautiful anti-music – clumsy and subtle compositions that find harmony in the most meagre conditions. A fitting and moving soundtrack for a reunion with Dundee.

I almost drift into a dream, saved only by the lack of public benches.

I break the spell and head to the escalator. I head up to the vestibule, clinging to the rubber handrail *-with tears in my fingers*. As I exit the station, I am hit with the moist force of Dundee's characteristic haar – the gloomy sea fog that often envelopes the town. There are two distinct modes of weather here, we like to brag about our status as Scotland's 'sunniest city' and it is true that the Dundee sky regularly showcases a glorious light show – with sweeping bands of pink, purple and orange clouds illuminated by the demanding sun. This is not the full story, and as today, the sea fret can be an overwhelming presence – transforming the seafront into the backdrop of a folk horror film or an American noir.

I pass by The Steeple Church outside of the Overgate. I am in the mood for some Thomas Dick inspired cosmic speculation, and a visit to a church does much for the imagination. The Steeple, however, gives me supreme anxiety. I don't know what it is, but it does little to provide me with the sanctuary this agnostic would expect from a place of worship – it could be the monstrously overgrown nature of the building, with three separate churches engulfed within one colossal structure. It could be the burden of history - the knowledge that The Steeple has served the city's worshippers for far too

many centuries to accommodate a non-believer
such as myself, the image of the city's last defenders
taking refuge there amidst the slaughter of the siege
of Dundee. Or most likely – it's the close vicinity
to the Overgate shopping mall that bothers me,
wrapping itself around the back of the church as a
ubiquitous boa constrictor. I have just returned from
Milan after all, where I was greatly disturbed by
the symbiotic relationship between capitalism and
Christianity. The extortionate entry fees charged
to visit historic churches, the long waiting list to
look upon The Last Supper of Leonardo da Vinci,
and the city's abundance of expensive art galleries
where devotional paintings are housed alongside
fascist, futurist compositions. This was all captured
in one single image – the Duomo, one of Europe's
most beautiful cathedrals, lit up at night and
projected upon as a gigantic Samsung advert. Milan
is an incredible city nonetheless, but I can't take The
Steeple with the Duomo on my mind – I need to
head to a church much more obscure, one with an
imagined history rather than a real one.

I leave the city-centre and head up to the
Hilltown, a pilgrimage that presents a substantial
challenge in my current condition. Each day we're
one step further into Hell. My destination is St.
Salvador's Episcopal Church – one of Dundee's best
kept secrets. The church was designed by G.F. Bodley

for the mill workers of the Hilltown – and it has a unique look. Bodley was a leading proponent of the Gothic Revival and a friend of William Morris. The church reflects the neo-medieval aspirations of its creator. I arrive to find an eerie quiet, and I take a seat on a pew in the back corner. A friendly nod from a priest as he goes about his business, and I settle in. The overwhelming red hue of the church's interior is at once troubling and calming. As I close my eyes to reflect, the red lingers in my retina – warning me of danger but offering a longevity that comforts me. Before long, I'm asleep.

With Dante on the mind, and the warm red décor all around me, it isn't long before I am dreaming of inferno. The hangover encourages a restless and uneasy sleep, an exploration of the Hells and Purgatories and Heavens I have inside of me. I wasn't raised within the church – I have no Catholic or Protestant hell in mind, no Presbyterian or Episcopal or Anglican stamp has been left on my consciousness. I avoided subjugation from the Metropolitan Church of Art of Jesus the Conductor. But whether or not they exist, we're slaves to the gods. My hell is amalgamated from poems, novels, art, and cinema. My hell is as much James Young Geddes as it is Dante. My hell is John Milton, Hieronymus Bosch, and Robert Garioch. My hell is classical, medieval, modernist, and post-nuclear. Dreams are always situated in our surroundings though, always populated with the faces we've seen before – thus my hell has a distinctly Scottish feel, a scorching tartan-coated shortbread-tin with a deafening soundtrack of screaming bagpipes.

It's not Virgil who acts as my guide, instead it is a man dressed in a shabby overcoat. A man with a solemn, sallow face and fish-like eyes. He greets me, descending from a pool of aboriginal slime – it is only when he grips my hand that I recognise William Topaz McGonagall. One look at him and I am already despairing of humanity. I am dejected even before we commence our tour of the Caledonian abyss. William has our final destination in mind, so we quickly bypass the first five circles. A castle populated by Kenneth MacAlpin and all the kings that came before. All seated around a large table in slumber, anticipating an endless slaughter: they ken-na the fear of God as they sleep ayont sin.

We're then trapped in a howling storm, blowing all those that succumb to lust in an infinite hochmagandist tornado. I spot Byron, Burns, and Mary Shelley caught among the tempest: man and woman know from birth that all voluptuousness is to be found in evil.

We approach a high tide of local delicacy feeding a colony of gluttons, gluttons feasting on congealed chip-shop fare under the supervision of a three-headed demonic westie: mortal food, as may dispose him best, for dissolution wrought by Sin.

We then come across a joust of greedy jute barons battling with colossal jute sacks full of gold. Glendale himself is proving to be the victor.

Feeling weary from our travels, I am glad when we approach a galleon that will carry us along the Tay and into the city. Our boatman is a frostbitten Falcon Scott, and he rows us along a frozen river populated by tyrannical kings and wrathful financial creditors – with the boat dragged along by his trusted huskies. Hunger and fear are the only realities in dog life, an empty stomach makes a fierce dog.

O the horror, o the humanity! When will I wake from this monstrous nightmare? We are greeted at the waterfront by a heretical welcoming committee – I see Knox, Calvin, and Beaton. I see the three Wedderburns chained to the front of the train station. I have to push myself through a sea of Buchanites: to think about God is to disobey God.

At Slessor Gardens there is an even greater crowd – a veritable Glastonbury of sin. The front row is like the advancing line of an army – a schiltron of shields and spears that William and I somehow manage to cut through as he waves some sort of official pardon: there is no document of civilization that is not at the same time a document of barbarism.

As we navigate the crowd I must ignore all manner

of whisperings – lies, rumours, flattery, and attempted
seductions. We are almost swallowed whole several
times, but William succeeds in pulling me through
a scrum of political councillors. We reach the Caird
Hall, and I can breathe again.

After the madness of the masses, the empty square
is almost tranquil. It seems too good to be true. A
graceful *piazza*, abandoned. Almost a painting by de
Chirico. William tells me we are approaching the
tenth circle, of which Dundee is the sole national
example. One that, he says, we share only with a
select few cities – the Prague of Kafka, Calvino's
Venice, the Lisbon of Fernando Pessoa. McGonagall
has been silent for most of this journey, now he is
recounting his tale with an abject joy. He dances
with glee as he gives me a rhyme:

The tenth circle of hell is a monument to absurdity
To all of this city's contradictions, to all I've seen
collapse, fall away, and leave Dundee
To every shell that stands,
every wasted opportunity
From the slums and the schemes, to the Magdalen
    Green

Let us build beautiful cinemas, and make them
    bingo halls
An abundance of theatres, housing nothing at all

Let's make all aware of our journalism, our jute, and
    our jam
Then condemn all three industries to be damned

So many churches, so little worshippers
So many hotels, so little guests
So many office blocks, no office workers

The worst city poet who ever lived,
and therefore, the best.

Paul Malgrati

Siege o Dundee, Circa.1651

The Howff awauks aneath the final leaf
that fell aff fae nae tree. Counsel bins
hae burst their wame under the weight o Stagecoach
receipts —scaittert athort the yaird wi cheap

French frehs deals on their backs. Banes
o lang deid men outcrop wi swaggerin
virr (they wad hae made some buzz, lang
syne, but nae ane's left tae tak tent).

Nae faur the greetin o guns is astoondin
General Monck's rockets hae kicked the MacManus
—blastit open— as Rabbie's heid and Victoria's

briests roll doon the crammasy stairs
in grim-like whigmaleerie. Dundee, the day,
is a bald quarry —an nae tree's left tae bide

The Law is a daft bairn wha's tint his bonnet
in a raid —the Memorial's fallen yestreen an naeb'dy
can mind the names, malfoustert athort the hill.
There's nae agenda fir Remembrance the day

as the gillies o Montrose mak their last staund
an fire their DEW at the DCA
(the roondheids' HQ) whaur the winners o Naseby
are watchin NBA atween twa salvos.

Ower by, the uni lab shelters twa IT
doctors. They scrieve in binary tae prove the dooble
predestination is algorithmically

soond an send puritan emails wi plenty
Cc nut nae Bcc —fir they ken they cannae
hide their herts fae God —or fae Trident for a' that.

This efternuin, anither missile's wrackit doon
the Owergait —the hail mall's heilster gowdie
wi Starbucks milkshakes in Debenhams bras
an Bobby Broon eenshadaes in Sportdirect snorkels.

There's e'en a pile o Tui postcairds crush't
By a squad o rollin baked tatties fae Fehv
Guys, rollin an bouncing on Lush bath bombs,
An Primarks breeks, an Tapman's tailor dummies,

rollin an bouncing under a snaw o condoms
fallen oot fae Boots, an yon crood o stairvin seagous
flytin ower bings o cookies, coffee cups, saund

stanes, braidbands, bricht purple plugs,
O2 4G 5Ss, an guts o gaffers
Wha wadnae flee a mall unner siege.

Ootside struts Fast Eddie —harmonica
daft an ayebidan gaberlunzie.
He daunders by, atween debris, yaulin
his tune, an kicks the kyte o Despairt Dan

—mad-like— intae the Caird Haa Colonnade.
"Anither brick in the wa", brags Eddie lad.
The square is his —glorious, jolly beggar!
Alane 'mang shrieks an grue an gloom.

He kicks aboot an blaws his tune —heel—
—tae— Eddie dances —heel—tae—dances awa
intae the haar o toxic gas that raxes,

aneath the hail o mortar shells that waltz,
Eddie dances —heel—tae—dances apairt,
his harmonies are grenades in the cranreuch o war.

Upstairs, in the crummlin Steeple, Dundee Coonsel
his gaithert. Gut-scared baillies, they ken
their end is near. Monck is comin! Roondheids
are ramming agin the door! The toon's a desert,

a coupon, a blank page, a wrackit utopia!
But time is left fir a last —hopeless— tryst.
A last minute reconstruction chart.
A Cooncilor's dream! A post-war Renaissance!

"Wheesht!" They say. "Hearken tae the Provost's
plan!
A Brutalist, Le Corbusist, Kumaistic,
criss-crossit, béton-holic, bald

square-gane, car-pairked, bingo-
-perked conurbation!" "Hear! Hear!
A toast, gentleloons, gie's a tart o concrete".

Doonstairs —slauchter— bluid an grue in the best
Scottish brew. Lo! Thae bings o bodies
in the Malmaison atween malagroused McEwan's
cavaliers. Lo! Thae bemangit bairns greetin

an stumbling thro moors o stumps on Union Street.
Lo! Thae skaithed quines, nailed an impaled
on the Mercat Cross. They shriek an oorie cruin
that minds o wives gaun aff the railway

—that silent crood o lasses that ne'er spake but tae
dree.
Aawhaur, suddron sodgers are mirthful wi murther.
Bluitert tae the bane, they burn, an grind, an butch,

an scramble, an reive, an rape, an slash, an mangle.
Heich up, on the tap o tanks, they upload photies
an close-up snaps o their mess on the Dark-Net.

Eastward, on Candle Lane, three Inglis sodgers
hae pit doon their Iphones. Englamoured wi gore,
their unco faces arena lauchin onymair.
The tane's a skybald squire fae the braes o Kent,

there's a sleekit look tae him, wi sair, mirky
eebas an a daf neb. The tither's a Warwick
dwairf —his bircht, purpie lips hings
lofty o'er his acrylic chin. The last yin's

a toothless Cockney wi Lilburne tattooed on his
airm
an the blood o Dundee burghers drippin fae his
Kevlar
(a Leveller wi post-traumatic stress disorder).

On the cobbles, a sairy sicht hae shoogelt their een:
a drouthy, nakit, woundit weans is suckling
dreh milk on his deid mither' briests.

"O visage familiers", said the squire,
"I mind thy face —thy tufted brows—as I
Killed thou, last night, in a daze of medifinil,
My blades in thy exhausted complexion, last night,

When I sliced and slained, your eyes in my eyes —
hideous
Thou wouldn't cry —I mind— I wouldn't cease,
Too blithe to spare —insipid like my lord,
Back home, in the stable, when he'd shut

My sister's moans with his lust. How shall I repent?
I didn't see thy child. Mes excuses, madame.
Shall I finish my days unattended, foolish

On my deathbed, arrested by remorse at the fatal
hour?
O let me take it home! Let me raise thy child!
And let it kill me when I teach it your end."

"Shut thy murderous mouth", said the dwairf,
"There is no escaping our delightful fall,
Elected Persephones on amphetamines
We have raked this underworld, unrepentant,

And made it our own for a few gallant hours.
Forget thy stable; forget thy land, thy kin!
We live in the rot of those we killed —thou belong
Here, in the tomb of her womb you dared to dig.

I bide in Dundee, forever alive in the corpses
I caused —in those unborn, ingrown, blessed
By the dry rhapsody of my sterile sword.

We've fed this soil with countless, scarlet offspring,
They are our children —freed from any spring. A
cheer
To them: our Tayside semination!"

"No!", the Cockney howl't, "There shall be no
Respite for none of us, no comforting thoughts.
Never will we eschew Dundee's dusky swallows.
Ever repeated nightmares, ever rising

Madness —this is our forever lot. No respite.
This town has birthed our bane —the blossom of
death
In our ketamined mirth. This child will curve
Our smiles, splatter our pride, spoil our wine

Colour of whines, estrange every single joy.
No respite, no hope, no life after Dundee.
I feel the stumps of my preys sprouting in me,

Into that empty soul I vomited long ago.
No respite —see the tide of our malign deeds.
Doomed murderers. The curse is final."

So speaks he, suddent, an pours his machine-gun
on his wabbit freens. Deid fall they on the wynd
—their bluid colloguin wi the cauld lass's wounds.
In a furious, dumfoonert dwam, the Cockney kneels,

an lifts the lifeless pieta intae his khaki airms.
Southward, tae the Tay, gangs he aghast,
past the corpse-filled quays an the haunted
heichway —past the moonscape o Slessor Gardens.

By the Tay, in a quate, goreless haven o a bay.
There, faur gane in lustless despair,
he digs a muckle grave fir the mither an wean.

'Tis tweelicht, when, his feet deep in the tangerine
saund, his faith ablaze wi a dreich hert,
he draws his gun an blaws his harns oot.

Doon by the beach, in the pooder o the nicht,
flickers the wreck o a bow-like craig o concrete.
Its cliff-edges hae crummelt doon the firth
—bombed tae bits— an its quirky cargo is scaittert

on the banks. A thrawn exhibition, it is,
wi trendy debris an fashionable splinters,
tartan rags an tweedy coupons twirlin
an curlin aroon the weet driftroom o Charles

Rennie Mackintosh. The orra biggin
mourns its pomp —gallus nae mair— an sinks
slowly in the daurk flood. Machine-guns

are mutterin awa tae firmament. Their souch faas
back o'er the hills an thaws intae psalms o sloom.
Sepias o piety drip in the riverbed.

Erin Farley

She Is A Problem Still

"The Dundee millgirl... Fifty years ago she was a problem, and she is a problem still."

- Reverend Henry Williamson, The People's Journal, 14 October 1922.

Dundee dominated Britain's textile industry, being dominated by it in return. During the nineteenth century, mills grew large and loud, the city spilled over its tiny medieval boundaries, and hundreds came seeking work. By the late Victorian era, most of those employed in the jute mills were women. It was said that the women's small nimble hands were better suited to this sort of work, and besides, they could be paid significantly less than men. Dundee quickly gained a reputation as a "woman's town". Women were the majority of the workforce, but they held little of the power. They were labour. All the mill owners, bosses, overseers – all the office staff but for a handful of typists – were men. On the factory floor, women signed to each other in the deafening clatter of the machines. Simple messages, marking the time until their next short break. A hand at the throat signified the overseers' approach. This meant to communicate the image of a collar and tie, but it also looks like choking, silencing. The noise made by mill workers was the subject of much disapproval

from the well-meaning respectable commentators of
the town, their laughing and talking in groups in the
streets and their songs during the strikes.

In the second half of the twentieth century,
the mills emptied as the industry moved to India.
Dundee's historic relationship with India is one
thread in a bloodstained colonial tapestry, and still
rarely spoken of in our remembering of Juteopolis.
The last mill in Dundee closed its doors for the
last time in 1994. The buildings remained, and
many remain still. Straight, solid buildings, rows of
windows, sun soaking in the industrial brickwork.
After these mills closed, with no immediate other
use, several lay empty. Dark inside, machines taken
out and shipped off, but debris with no monetary
value still scattered on the floor.

I am descended on my father's side from jute mill
workers. My granny was one of eleven children, most
of whom were girls and most of whom worked in
mills. It left a mark on generations of Dundee women,
with hearing so damaged that doctors looked in vain
for head trauma in their notes, fingers and hands
mangled or gone, skin on necks worn to paper from
years of carrying stacks of chemical-soaked fibre
under their chins. My great-aunt, Florrie, once told
me about her sister's injury at work. "She lost hauf
her hand tae the machine belt. The boss says dinny
worry, ye've got a job for life. She says so what's ma

job noo? He says, cleanin the toilet." She left the mill after that.

I tended towards the ghostly as a child, seeking it and fearing it in equal measure. I remember, in pieces, the walk back from my grandmother's house near Balgay Park. On the way to the train station we must have passed many of these old mills, but I remember Logie Works. I only remember it in the dark, jagged broken glass reflecting orange streetlamps around the edges of black windows. This was the Coffin Mill. It is named for its shape, with two long buildings running parallel to one another, then leaning in towards one another, a third linking them lengthways. From above, the lines run like those of a coffin. The two long buildings are linked by a narrow iron bridge.

I was somehow always aware that this building was haunted. The ghost was of a woman who had once worked there. I imagined her pale presence in that darkness, trailing hair in the dusty corners of the mill. The ghost appeared on the bridge sometimes, the story went – her white form made shaky steps until halfway, then she toppled and fell down to the courtyard. She was a well-established legend. People had seen her.

Ideas fragment when they are let loose: she is many people, many deaths. Her husband fell into a boiling tank at his work in another mill. Unable to cope with her grief she threw herself from the bridge, leaving Dundee seven more orphans. No, she was pulled into a machine when her hair got caught, or she lost her arm and couldn't work, rather than go to the poorhouse she jumped to her death. She died trying to save a child who was in danger on the bridge. Now she glides over the rusted hole in the middle of it. Other mills are haunted by victims of industry too. Late workers at West Ward Works were told to listen for the heavy footsteps of someone who never clocked out.

One story goes more or less like this. She was a young women, barely more than a child, like many in the mills, who took a job in Logie Works to support her younger siblings. Her mother was dead and her father unemployed. One of the mill overseers began to give her preferential treatment, giving her first choice of overtime hours, saying he understood her difficult position. One night when the machinery had been shut down and the mill was quiet, he locked her in his office and he raped her. She kept coming back to work, because what else could she do, and she stopped having periods and she fainted at her machine. She went to see him, to tell him she was pregnant – what was he going to do? Gossip was already spreading. The overseer told her to meet him on the bridge when her shift had finished, so they could talk. He had no intention of being named as the father of her child. He threw her from the iron bridge to her death.

She was killed, but she could not be made invisible. At nights she walks along the bridge still, pausing halfway, and falling again and again. A reminder, a marker of conscience for the society which set it up to happen.

Did that really happen?

It was true for someone.

...is still true.

Our ghosts are often painful reminders of the things done to women in the name of keeping them quiet and saving men's reputations. Most often, though, these white ladies are of better breeding than our Coffin Mill Girl, now reduced to charming tourists at Glamis in artfully stained gowns. We see them as white for innocence, red for blood, neither of which is the entirety of their meaning.

But ghosts cannot be killed, and folklore gives agency to the story itself.

In 1945, she returned.

On Wednesday the 5th September, the Dundee Courier reported that, "according to one old woman who resides in the neighbourhood, the ghost of that worker, who through the years has become known as 'The White Lady,' visits the old mill at intervals. Last night the news spread through the district that she had [...] been seen crossing the bridge that joins two sections of the mill." She brought chaos. The police arrived to find a large crowd at the gates of the mill clamouring to see her. They were shouting, throwing stones, causing much damage to property. And what of it, it is only property, after all? The street shone with broken glass. A policeman and the works watchman walked around the building, shining torches into every dark window. "There is no ghost," they told the crowd. "Go home. There is no such thing as a ghost."

The 1940s were a reasonably profitable time for jute, though the industry was clearly in decline compared to the heady days of the nineteenth century. It went on, though. Although the Coffin Mill had since been turned into a furniture-makers, other jute mills in the city kept up with the times. Safety was, officially, at an all-time high: no more child labour, a record low of fatal accidents. One of the respondents to the Dundee Oral History Project, interviewed in 1985, recalled her working life in the mid-twentieth century. Bigger machines which could do more with less operatives were being installed. The workers on these machines were less likely to lose a hand, but had to stretch and contort themselves more in order to cover a larger work area. She remembered an increase in the number of pregnant workers who miscarried as these machines were introduced.

It was true for someone.

Ghost stories are about our most live worries. In The Idea of North, Peter Davidson wrote that ghost stories flourish in times and places where two distinct belief systems exist and overlap. Victorian Britain was undoubtedly one of these places, as an increasing faith in developing industry and technology jostled with a deep-seated religious belief which touched on every aspect of life. The belief systems involved need not be strictly religious. Many ghost stories are about anything but death and the soul. In Dundee, the woman as worker co-existed with the woman as caregiver and homemaker. They were scrutinised in their behaviour on the street, that place which – neither home nor work – they could be only themselves for a brief time. Their public behaviour was analysed through rivers of newspaper ink. Either dangerous, corrupting, loud, drunken viragoes, or hardworking innocents, permanently on the verge of becoming a victim. The poet Joseph Lee saw their tired faces in the first years of the twentieth century and lamented:

This haunted thing that labours like a brute
(As seeming patient, and as sadly mute)
For what? – some sorry shreds of sacking jute!
And that alone.

Having an illegitimate child was of course frowned upon by church and state, but in practice, of course it happened, and people dealt with it. Among the mill communities of Victorian Dundee, many unmarried women had children. The rules of industry, the rules of capital, used social expectations as a mask, but the poor could have all the bastards they wanted as long as they did not threaten the hierarchy of class and gender. What killed the girl of the Coffin Mill was not that she could not exist as an unmarried pregnant woman – it was that the father of her unborn child was her superior, and she could not be trusted to shut up about it. She threatened to break her unwritten contract of compliance.

That's what you get.

But the women of Dundee were not resigned to be these sorry haunted things. In the telling of a story, the singing of a song, stories become multiple. She could become not white lady but poltergeist. She could cause someone to consider joining the strike. She could make a mill boss sleep a little less easy at night after hearing the women's clattering tongues grow quiet as he walked by. She could cause rocks to be thrown through the windows of a mill, sixty years or more after her death. They were told to be quiet, but they filled the streets with noise.

On the 22nd of October 1892, the Dundee Evening Telegraph reported on disruptions during a Royal Visit to the city:

"A body of young girls on strike from a neighbouring mill made matters interesting by parading up and down between the High Street and the Tay Bridge Station, singing a "strike" song with the dreary and unmusical refrain of:
Hey-o, hey-o, we'll get a heicht o wages o!"

Dundee mill culture in the 19th and early 20th centuries was a youth culture and a women's culture. This annoyed male would-be trade union leaders to no end. These young women who were told their place was at a mill then in the home and never in-between, who worked twelve-hour days and then came home to cook and clean and sew, endless stitches consuming their lives, they spread whispers through the mills. A strike could come about in a matter of hours and it was heralded by song. An Evening Telegraph journalist in 1899 wrote with foreboding:

"All this forenoon I have heard the strike song

resounding through the Dundee streets, and I am
afraid this local Carmagnole presages trouble. So far
the younger folks have been taking the active lead in
this strike business..."

> We are out for higher wages
> As we have a right to do
> For we have a right to live
> As well as you

Strikes were carnivals of resistance. Women work
masks and banged drums. They played games, girls'
clapping games, where sometimes they would
surround a policeman, make him the involuntary
subject of a narrative which hinged on the girl's
power to choose a partner★. They encircled, and
danced, and created a space which was neither work
nor home and entirely women's. They sang.

> Three times around went our gallant gallant ship,
> and three times around went she
> Three times around went our gallant gallant ship,
> and she sank to the bottom of the sea

The story of the Coffin Mill girl has been with me
a long time, in different versions, holding different
meanings. I tell it, rarely. It is the most difficult
story of all those I know to tell. It probably never

happened, not in the way we need for history to have happened to be 'real'. We will never find her name on a register, black mark ink fading. But the first time I got up the courage to tell her story at a public storytelling session, a woman in the audience came up to me after. She said something to me which I have always remembered.

"Thank you for telling that. It was true for someone."

These stories, the ghosts that haunt us and resurface after generations, do not say: this is what happened, exactly as it happened, with dates and records. They say: this is true. This is a thing many people have lived, it is true, and it is important. They say, it's not just you. They say, listen, we are many, and we will not be silenced.

But ma line's as good as ony and Eh'm very proud to say
It was fae a Dundee weaver that Eh came

We are a problem still.

★Siobhan Tolland's excellent PhD thesis, "'Jist ae wee woman': Dundee, the Communist Party and the feminisation of socialism in the life and works of Mary Brooksbank," (University of Aberdeen, 2005) looks at how this became a part of a truly female-centric radical tradition in the twentieth century, through the frame of the life and work of Mary Brooksbank.

Andy Jackson

Talos Over Tayside

This city harbours many minor Titans,
built into the buttresses of tenements,
cast in bronze, or poured like concrete
into bridge supports. I am one of them;
mythic yet enlightened, elusive,
though familiar as elements of brick and burn.

I've many names; you can call me Talos,
creaking giant, scourge of Argonauts,
and I will eat this city, one postcode at a time,
then wade into the river, lift a fleeing ship
out of the Tay, shake its crew like salt
across the Sidlaws, and use it as a toothpick.

Let the earth quake as I pass,
let the shops and houses crumble into snow
until there's not a single building left alive.
When the dust clears you will know
that what a place is truly made of will survive.

Billy Bytheway

It caught ye aince again; that same dwam –
just eight, doon Mornin Noon & Nicht
fir messages – ten-pack o Lambert & Butler –
bare-scud save yir sister's baffies,
naebdy saying naethin; aa lookin away.

Yon's yir faither wi his heavy an his dram
at thi bar like a coo hingin ower a dyke,
haufway atween thi howff an thi gutter,
a ghaist amang thi schemies an thi scaffies,
abdy swallyin thir ain gless o waes.

An ye, wha life nudges alang like a laum
tae thi skemmels, blint by the licht,
smearin oan the lippy like it's butter,
tryin oan yir mither's voice, thi way she laughs
at aa thi stupit hings yir faither says,

ye huvna realised thi time has cam
tae step oot thi museum o yir mind an ficht
fir whit yir chyngin intae. Open up thi shutters,
cut thi labels fae the dress an jist be happy
that yir aywis wha ye are in yir ain claes.

Anna Stewart

Gisilberht and Jorge Visit the Wellgate Centre, Dundee

At the entrance to the Wellgate Centre in Dundee
city's High Street, Gisilberht and I pause to listen
to the clattering doors, the footfall and squeaky
wheels; a shiny toy car drones its pretend motor and
a television plays rolling news. We also hear voice,
the local dialect has maintained its strength and the
song of it rings out all around us. Gisilberht claps to
the rhythm of our new surroundings and I compose
notes in my moleskin journal. A perfumery sits to
our left and I follow Gisilberht as he peers through
the windows at boxes of smells – the shiny packaging
and eroticised images. Beckoning me over with the
energy he usually displays in times of creative fervour,
Gisilberht encourages me to widen my nostrils.

"Sniff Jorge, open your nose to this stuff, just
sniff!"

I'm at once immersed in aromatic waters, heart
notes of sandalwood and head notes of coconut. We
stand together in this place surrounded by the sillage
of liquid wax and ethanol watching the faces of the
people, and I experience the deep vibrations of what
it means to be a common man. A shop assistant steps
out from behind a glass counter and approaching us
asks if we need any help, to which I reply,

"We're merely enjoying your air."

Which is of course the purpose for our journey: to ' the scent, the sonic, the visuals of this building and the people in it, for this is the true centrepiece of the city of Dundee.

As we approach the television, we're again engaged in conversation but this time with two men both wearing t-shirts with the word Sky emblazoned on their backs. They ask if we have Sky television, and I assure them that we do not. They encourage us to hear about their latest package and intend on offering us a deal until I inform them that we don't live locally but are merely visiting for the day in order to ascertain some sense of this shopping centre erected on the historic site of the Wellgate Steps. The gentlemen both understand our purpose but encourage us to go online on our return home to peruse the deals they're offering and they give us their names repeatedly, and their cards. I ask them, incidentally, if they have any information on the building and one of them recalls visits as a child and informs us of the now expunged waterfall feature where he had the happy occasion to throw half-pence coins for luck while his Mother was shopping.

The other gentleman tells us about a time when he and his school friends stole a cassette from Virgin Records and two security guards chased him down the High Street until unfortunately, he was captured and brought back to the Wellgate to return the

album which he precisely recalls being R.E.M.'s
Automatic for the People. Local police and his
parents were informed and he was banned from the
centre for over a year. While he recounts this tale we
listen with great interest and I record his narrative
on Dictaphone while Gisilberht adorns a black
hood and re-enacts the scene with his collection of
Bunraku puppets. It's impossible to say the effect of
such an experience on a young mind but as this man
tells us his story I see in his features the excitement
and pleasure of that chase, and behind his eyes I
witness a flicker of loss. Now in middle age, he stands
day after day in the place where he was caught mid-
flight in a bid for freedom after an act of theft during
his youth. It appears to us to be a very unfortunate
tale given his current position, and for our London
exhibition we have decided to present his story with
the melancholic slant it deserves, as though this man
has been imprisoned in the Centre forever.

On the next floor we come across an eatery
called Muffin Break. Here, we have a clear view
of the outlying shops and passers-by so decide to
allow ourselves time to sit. Gisilberht orders a pot of
earl-grey for two, and we find it interesting that we
receive individual mugs of not-quite boiled water
from which we're obliged to extract teabags with
wooden sticks. It's then we hear the first chimes of
the infamous Wellgate Clock situated on the floor

above us. I crane my neck and am able to see one of the little doors flap open. Had we not just sat down, I would have been inclined to travel the short escalator ride to witness the midday ding dong of all twelve nursery rhymes; the waking lion, the prancing unicorn, and the gun-toting-fiddle-playing-vodka-drinking cat on hind legs loved by the children of Dundee since the clock's installation in 1978. However, we agree the journey unnecessary because of the numerous Youtube videos of the clock we've already seen. And because, as part of this project we've purchased the Charles Anderson design drawings and engaged with a clockmaker whose been building a replica in our London studio three times the size of the Wellgate original. On a personal note, the building of this replica has become a matter of dispute between Gisilberht and I – it was he who insisted the clock become part of our installation, but it is he who has since developed a deep (and in my view unwarranted) hatred for the clockmaker.

Gisilberht thrusts a fork-full of baked goods in my direction. "Taste this, it's warm Jorge and really tastes like pie, even though it's not pie."

He eats a banoffee muffin, but my abhorrence of sweet treats prohibits sharing. I watch whitish-yellow crumbs roll from his mouth to jumper, and notice the star shaped pattern he's creating on the red wool stretched across his stomach. For Gisilberht every moment produces something new, art pours out of him and to have had the privilege to spend my days in the shadow of his imaginative power has been wonderful. I hastily uncap my camera lens and take a succession of photographs, which will be available on our website under the Series Category: Nutrient Substances, Subcategory: Out and About, Location: Wellgate Dundee, Entitled: Gisilberht Jumpermuffin Crumb Star/Banoffee.

Towards the back of the building (or the front, depending which way you come at the thing) is a set of inconspicuous double doors – a fire exit that's been camouflaged by paint a similar colour to the walls. We want to get into the bowels of the building and decide, without permission, to push the doors open. On doing so, we come upon the most wonderful sight – two girls of sixteen or seventeen are dressed as clowns and sitting on the floor by a helium canister. One of the girls is filling shiny metallic balloons the shape of Disney characters with said helium, and the other is leaning against the stone wall of the dingy corridor, smoking a cigarette and watching the balloons inflate. Both look perfectly miserable and the sadness behind their painted smiles adds to the macabre quality of the scene. They lift their eyes towards us and stare. We hover in the doorway attempting to imprint the shape, colour and feel of the moment into our consciousness until we realise that we're not at all welcome and so with reluctance (but in some haste) we make our retreat.

It's at that moment we happen upon a woman holding a mop, sweeping back and forth behind us, Gisilberht almost stands on her. He apologises and explains our purpose for being in this out-of-bounds area. She says she doesn't mind as she has no particular authority in the Centre, her role is simply to clean the raw sewage from the designated patches of ground prescribed to her on the "wee" plastic map attached to her lanyard, these are the zones in which the duct tape and white emulsion has not successfully sealed the forty-year old pipes. She informs us that she herself was once an artist and I can see from her mop strokes that we are in the company of a restless soul. She tells us about a commune she lived in with her Croatian friend in London in the early 2000s, at the time when we ourselves were experimenting with bodily fluids on canvas in the same city. She informs us that she saw our show at the Tate Modern and loved it, in parts. I wonder about the other parts but decide not to probe the matter further. The notes I've made on our conversation will follow in the style of a monologue:

Donald Henry

Simon...someone

"How are you going to get down, Kelvin?"

A moment's thought: that's what he hadn't given that. Fight or flight: an instinctive reaction; an involuntary reflex. Battle or bottle, and you couldn't fight the Polis, not now they had the tasers. Look at the bastards sideways you'd be on your back wi' your fillings bursting oot your teeth like popcorn.

Aye, fight or flight, and if you couldn't fly, then climbing was the next best thing, because they couldn't get you: Health and Safety, and the German Shepperd's no' been born could climb a tree.

"Why don't you come down, Kelvin?"

"You fat baldy bastard. Why don't you go and get a coffee and a fucking doughnut, because I'm not coming down!... D'you think this is fuckin' funny? You'll no' think it's funny when I hit you in the eye wi' a fuckin' acorn!"

"You'll have to climb an oak tree to find acorns, Kelvin; those are pine cones."

"In that case, you'd better go and cone aff the road!"

Nah, you'd have to be mental to fight the Polis, and he wasn't mental, just played up to it. Well, she'd come to expect it. Imagine calling them on him again. She'd had that door reinforced too. He'd only wanted to see his bairns. Past their bedtime? ...they had a right to see their father.

"You've left your bag down here…"

"I know. D'you think I don't know whaur I've left ma bag? How could I climb a fucking tree wi' that?" Well alright, after he'd seen the bairns, he thought he might have slept on the settee. But there was nae need for what she'd said,

"Dinnae think you're movin back in here." Just cos he'd showed up wi a bag. That was fuckin' typical: suspicious. "Maniac!"? She'd be a fuckin' maniac, if she'd been knocked back by the hostel, just for havin' a couple o' pints. He'd give them "drunk".

"Come down now, and we can get this sorted." The gentle touch, eh?

"Is that your partner?"

"I'm really worried, Kelvin." He's thirty foot up a tree, and she's worried. "It's really dangerous."

"Your Mum's disappointed in you…"

"If you come down now, we can get you into court in the morning."

"…your mum's disappointed in you, because you're in the Polis, and your partner is a skinny prick."

"I thought I was a fat bastard?"

"Well now, you're a skinny, fucking prick!"

"If you don't come down soon, it'll be too late to get you called in the morning, and you'll be in the cells over the weekend."

"I'd rather do three months in Perth than a weekend in Bell Street; it's a fucking shit-hole."

The Firies, now, "Have you rung for a ladder? I'm no' a fuckin' cat! You know what you'll have to do now? You'll have to call out Special Branch."

"We might have to bring back the birch for you, Kelvin."

"You fat bastard, you wouldn't know a joke if you found it in a Christmas cracker. And you'd better order a fucking pizza, because I'm not coming down!"

★

Could stay up here like that fella, lived on a column for thirty years; no' Jim Crumley, Simon… someone. Simon; hauled up food monks put in a basket. Never hear about his shite, though; must have had a bucket round the back: bread up, shite doon. Took a leak like that wee boy in Belgium.

★

"Hello, I'm Inga, and I'm a police officer. I would like to help you with your situation." Plain clothes, now.

"You don't sound like a police officer. Where do

you come from?"

"I come from Germany. Do you mind that I'm from Germany, Kelvin?"

"No, I've got nothing against Germans, but I hate fuckin' Nazis."

"I'm not a Nazi, Kelvin, I'm a police officer."

"Well, we'll no' split hairs."

"Kelvin, what led you to this?"

"She'll no let me see the bairns: her across the road…Aye, you! Close your blinds and get to your fuckin' bed."

"You know that there's an Anti-Harassment Order, Kelvin. You must go through your solicitor; you can't just show up at the door."

"It's my house. Hear that, you: my house! I bought you a car."

"Your children should not have to hear this, Kelvin."

"How's no', eh? Let them hear the truth. They've got to grow up sometime. Let them hear exactly what it's like, so they get the right idea."

"It's very late now; what about the neighbours…"

"What about them? Half the street are fuckin' alcys …Next-door neighbour, d'you want to buy a ticket, hen? I'm here all week!"

★

"Are you going to come down, now?"

"Aye, I'm going to come down."

"How are you going to get down, Kelvin?"

"Fuck knows…"

AR Crow

Kingsway Santa

We speak in letters and numbers
SBARs and early warning scores
letters and numbers too sparse

to encompass the feeling of just not quite right
or the look of the one who might die that night

this is no brave new world
all words are flawed yet
our senses may be better than X-rays

they call me with NEWS
one question implicit
what must we do?

high scores are no prize here
I hear no surprise when I say
I'll come straight away

Santa is wizened, his hat limply droops
tottering with frailty
failing mind, kyphotic stoop

oral intake has reduced they say
but we do not have the numbers

we weigh up fates in imperfect measures
letters and numbers and other ways

my senses say, Santa will not die today
when I touch him, he says

GET THOSE FUCKING HANDS OFF ME

Dundee Train Station 22/6/18

The new board is up
but the work is not complete
a space shines, empty
yet replete with possibility

two young guys walk before me
onto Riverside
arms round shoulders
bodies round the corner
and in through the side

a passing place
small but not too small for
lips to meet in the middle
with hard tenderness

and here
a kiss is more than a kiss
a kiss is more than a kiss is more than a kiss

sometimes
consecration comes
before the opening date

Mas que nada

You lit the beacons
down on Perth Road
a salt-rimmed glimmer
beckoned us to Mas

amidst this storm
a gathering place
for queers and straights

margaritas here
then food and wine
at your place
Cards Against Humanity
til late

when to laugh over
cards dealt to us
was the only way
to survive this game

E.G. Smith

On a winter afternoon, one Wednesday in Dundee, whilst eating lunch, I almost have a realisation about the role and use of technology in contemporary society, about how to transcend it, but then I don't.

"Let's go", says colleague, "to Seabrae gardens."

Sure, I say, let's go. It's our lunchbreak, and we have about thirty minutes to eat our wraps before we are forced back to work. We almost always walk down to Seabrae for our lunch. Colleague almost always suggests it. We walk, a moment, in silence.

"That sky looks like a Turner."

We're looking at the view as we approach the park. The sky opens up over the hills across the water. From this far back the hedge bordering the park conceals the dual carriageway as it passes the great supermarket. That was colleague by the way, and I rummage in my mind for something interesting to say.

"Last night I watched the sunrise over a mountain on Red Dead." Colleague waits for me to continue, so I do. "And I mean, it was really beautiful, you know, the colours and the scenery and everything." Colleague is still staring ahead, observing the sky. "And it struck me, as I watched, that I have never seen a sunrise for real. In actual real life. Like, gotten up early in the morning, and set out with the specific intention to watch the sunrise. I mean, I must have seen them before, on my way to places or whatever, but I'd never just done it, you know?"

It does, by the way. Look like a Turner. Clouds and sky merging through brushstrokes. We have more or less reached the crossing.

"It's a weird thing about video games", this is colleague again, "their drive for greater realism. It stands in opposition to the flow of other forms of Western Art. The development of art. Something it shares with Hollywood and 3D movies."

Yeah, colleague can be a pretentious cunt. We are passing by the monument to one of our city's Great Cultural Figures, and just beyond the bandstand I'm eyeing up our usual bench. It's unoccupied. Colleague continues on their speech. Just imagine me affirming and negating where appropriate through the next bit. Imagine me giving the appearance of following the argument with interest and understanding.

"The progression from realism, to the abstract, to the conceptual. That has been the flow of Western Art, moving from the thing, to a something, to the nothing of pure idea. But games have not been like that. I'm glad you mentioned Red Dead, because I have been thinking about the GTA series recently. Think about it. GTA started in the abstract, blocks and shapes of colour, that we read as thieves, murderers, car-jackers, and their tools. These blocks became more rounded, more defined, more real in the second game. The real jump though comes with GTA 3, that surreal environment of cubist polygons, silent protagonists, and the future bursting onto the horizon through busted-frame-rate pop-ups."

We are at the bench now. The bench faces the wrong way, our backs to the view. In front of us; the gardens, the road, the university campus. I bite into my wrap. Begin chewing slowly, as if ruminating on colleague's spiel. Please continue to imagine.

"And then from there we hit realism. GTA 4 was a realistic projection of reality. I recognised the cars. The scratches and dents. The violence became visceral. And then GTA 5, and although the narrative remains satirical, the virtual world itself is real. Your game with the sunrise is the next step in this progression, sitting alongside the development of VR headsets and the rest."

I mention colleague has missed a couple of releases and expansions across formats. That China Town Wars, for example, blurs their story somewhat. Colleague assures me that this isn't the point.

"The point", says colleague, "is that for Western Art the move into abstraction is a self-imposed constraint that drives the art forward. In video games, graphics are a materially-imposed constraint of the technology. Technology that slowly releases its grip on the designer, opening them up into realist forms of representation. Western Art is a journey from the material to the immaterial, to the purely conceptual. Video games are the reverse. For this reason, we can view VR as a way of bringing us back to the dirt of existence, the thingness of things, from the realm of ideas to the physical."

I continue to chew for a moment. Then swallow. Pause, and formulate my response.

"Yeah, you can even play it in first person. Red Dead I mean. Well, and GTA

but my words are stalled, and my eyes wrenched up, by a sudden and explosive sound. Wrap stands rigid in my tightened grip, mouth flapping open, and eyes staring. Something like a huge crate has fallen off the back of a flatbed, the truck lurched up onto the curb, and has busted open. Its lid split apart like a pair of barn doors. It takes my eyes a moment to resolve just what it is flowing between these.

Rodents. A roiling flow of mottled fur. Rats, or Guinea pigs, or something. Hundreds of them, pouring out of this crate. Colleague exclaims an "Oh No!", or something that sounds much like it, as a car travelling in the opposite direction slams down screeching brakes when confronted with the creatures. Several explode beneath the tires, bursting like some gore-filled water bomb.

Following instinctual sub-verbal communication, both colleague and I jump up onto the bench as the vermin charge first towards, and then beneath us. They are heading towards the sea. I look around me. See the animals burrowing in the flower beds, climbing up stone piles like stairways over the curb, rolling down the concrete steps. More than should be possible from a crate of that size, like some kind of illusion. A trick.

I notice, simultaneously, that what remains of my wrap is no longer in my hand, and that a swell of the rodents are viciously consuming those remnants. It's this sight, as the tide of creatures continues to flow beneath me, that I begin to have what I will later consider the start of a thought. Looking at the mad devouring of my lunch, a wooden spring-operated mouse-trap comes to mind. I think about how that trap comes to force its use, the bait a lure to encourage the mice – drawing them in. I remember playing video games as a kid. Seeing the traps and enemies, but staying idle as my avatars strolled toward them. Eager to see the death animations, the mulch they made of the characters. The obstacles, by their very existence, demand that they be used. The invention of the mousetrap demands, forces, the dead mouse. If only we could find a different way to reach the ch

"shit, gotta go". That's colleague again, jumping from the bench. The rats, or whatever they were, are past us now, flowing down the banks, towards the water, eliciting screaming in their wake. Crushed and trampled corpses are left strewn about the parks pathways, in devastated flower beds, spread across the road.

We are late for work. I think of this as I look at the monument, that figure shielding their eyes as they look into the future. Looking down the road. Looking in the wrong direction. Missing the creatures beneath our feet.

Miguel Alcázar

Something for your M.I.N.D.
or another irrelevant conversation at the
Harris Academy, Dundee, on a fine morning,
early March

"Hello, Alison!"

"Hi, Jane!"

"How are you doing this morning?"

"Not bad!"

"Have you done anything special this morning?"

"Uh-huh."

"Will you tell me about it?"

"Uh-huh."

"So …"

"So I just came from an appointment with the
school's careers adviser!"

"No way!"

"Oh, yeah!"

"And how did that go?"

"Just fine."

"The usual crap, huh?"

"Actually, not at all!"

"Oh, I see."

"Yep."

"Will you tell me about it, please?"

"Okay, so, basically, this guy goes and tells me
    …"

"Alison, I'm all ears."

"… that I could become an attractive drug-fuelled dancing queen, going out every day, making out with all the hot guys I'll be able to meet at the university's Union and at some local joints where they happen to play this new hipsterised version of nineties' techno and where everyone seems to be losing control of themselves day in, day out, acting as if they were but carefree versions of their primitive ancestors while receiving through their senses the myriad of psychedelic stimuli—fluorescent lights, fluorescent flavours, fluorescent smells!—that are being constantly thrown at them by someone making a huge profit out of them although, well, not a profit of the kind that can ruin your life and make you truly stellar and tubular, I mean, for the rest of your days."

"Hi, Alison"

"Hello, Jane"

"Have you done anything special this morning?"

"Yes, I was just telling you …"

"Have you done anything special this morning, then?"

"No."

"Today?"

"No."

"This week?"

"Shit, Jane, you're getting one of them seizures again, so I will just keep telling you the story of my visit to the effing adviser "

"Okay, Alison, fair enough."

"… and how I could choose to become someone, like, really successful, you know? Like spending all the time earning money and all, like, how much money did you make last minute, and actually being able to give you a number as an answer to that question, while eating something expensive and organic and gross in one of those restaurants I don't know anything about just yet but that are everywhere around Edinburgh, the Athens of the North, the place where I'm determined to live when I grow up, where I'm going to spend my days having the most of funs in an office the size of a whole building, mirrored walls, and whatever excites your imagination the most, all around the place, all the time."

"Hello, Alison,"

"Hey, Jane?"

"How ar eyo udo ing thism ornin g?"

"Oh, fuck."

"Wil lyo utel lmea bou titp, lease?"

"… a bohemian writer in sunny (way sunnier than Dundee) but somewhat depressing (of course, much less) Barcelona, Spain, where young people like to see themselves as belonging to the creative type even if they don't write, paint, direct, dance, or really do anything creative at all apart from wasting their hours, days and weeks working for companies that seem kinda cool—they do publishing stuff, digital marketing, supersuspensful avant-garde urban model strategic branding!—in what essentially are low-paid, soul-crushing jobs that will burn them through boredom and despair before they're thirty, a moronic fate I won't be sharing with them cause I'll be living the writer's life, drinking coffee and cocktails all the time, on those splendid and decadent *plazas*, under the shadow of those autumnal, Mediterranean trees …"

"Alison."

"… working on an impossible novel no one will ever publish but …"

"Alison."

"Hi, Jane!"

"You know you're the one to blame for us running in circles here, right?"

"How so?"

"Well, you and your fucking visit to the school's adviser this fucking morning …"

"I think that's not completely fair, Jane …"

"… carelessly opening endless possibilities within the reality both of us happen to be sharing at this school, at this very precise moment …"

"Well, you know what I should do, then?"

"What, you bitch?"

"Well, I may just have to become what my mom

and pops call *a normal person*, like all them people
who have regular jobs ranging from the very
boring to the extraordinarily okayish, and who
live in the suburbs the West End Broughty Ferry
Carnoustie Forfar Cupar Forpar Cufar Forfor! and
only drive to the city centre on the weekend to go
to the pub or to a fancy restaurant or to the cinema
or to the places where people of their kind usually
gather, carrying on with their lives in a discrete,
albeit tragic and ultimately meaningless, manner,
periodically replacing one another and working
towards the evolution of humanity as the most
dutiful workers on the face of the earth."

"Wow Alison, so many options there …"

"I know, right?"

"Like, how many lives can one go through in a
single life?"

"Uh-huh."

"It's really something for your M.I.N.D., eh?"

"It is, Jane. It really is."

Matt Townsend

BOXING DAY 2018, NEAR VICTORIA PARK

It's nearly midday before Minnie awakes. Nothing indicates it to be this late. The light coming through the window is a timeless grey. In the apartment everything is quiet. Minnie doesn't feel pangs of hunger despite missing her morning meal. Her stomach slightly bulges from the leftovers tipped into her plate around midnight. By reflex the thought of food enters her mind all the same. As far as she is aware her owner still sleeps in the bedroom down the hallway. If the door wasn't shut Minnie would try to wake her owner with or without hunger. She might still go and call from outside.

Minnie uncurls and lifts her head to survey the lounge room. Max lies asleep on the other end of the couch with his head tilted almost upside down and pulled towards his rising and falling chest. She looks at the stump where his hind leg used to be. It mystifies her. His tail rests still. He is in deep sleep. Minnie thinks about lying on top of him for warmth but the urge isn't strong. She's comfortable where she is.

Minnie begins washing her shoulder and moves down to her paw. She spreads her claws open and works on removing the worn nail husk using her back teeth. She can taste last night's turkey on her breath and is again reminded of her instinct to want food. She stops grooming and pricks her ears to listen for any movement. All she can hear from the direction of the bedroom is a dull snore.

Beginning with her upper body Minnie stretches and lifts herself up. She takes another look at Max and hops down onto the floor. Out of habit she checks her food bowl and finds nothing.

She is about to begin calling her owner from the hallway when she senses the more urgent need to relieve herself. She considers using the litter box but decides to hold on and hopefully go outside. Perhaps after being fed.

The thought of outside prompts her to cross the room and jump onto the ledge. She pulls back slightly when she feels the chill coming off the window pane. Outside reads cold and still. There is no sign of traffic at the normally busy intersection of Blackness and Balgay roads. There are no people on the sidewalks or any other creatures within sight. Everything is grey or dark with dampness.

Her head spins back at the distinct sound of the bedroom door. Her owner appears. Minnie emits an eager and petitioning meow as she bounds down from the ledge.

Nae ye dinnae, says the owner. Oot wi ye.

Minnie knows what's coming. She is scooped up by her owner whose other free arm opens the window. She drops outside.

Minnie lands and stands to attention. Her body twitches as it adjusts to the cold. She waits to see if Max will be put out too. She sniffs the air and listens to the world. The lack of activity is disconcerting. Max doesn't appear and the window is clamped shut. Minnie remembers her full bladder and trots away.

Normally she would take longer to choose between two directions. Towards Victoria Park avoids crossing Blackness Road but there is a higher risk of dogs. Given the absence of traffic she instead decides to brave a crossing and head towards Western Cemetery.

Although the road remains empty Minnie tenses upon approach. The memory of Max's accident almost two years ago still exists in her consciousness. The squealing of brakes. The yowl from Max. The smell of blood and burnt rubber. She has forgotten the connection she made with his stump when he returned from the vet. She only remembers the danger.

She slinks between two parked cars and observes the road. All is quiet. She waits another moment. Still nothing. An instinct of propulsion kicks in and she scurries across the road. She reaches the other side and keeps some momentum going in preparation for the next and slightly less daunting crossing. She turns down Balgay Road and dashes to the other side. She is safer now. Her body relaxes but she remains alert.

A gust hits her and her fur shudders and flattens. The air carries the familiar scent of the Tay River. She heads into Hillcrest Road which is more sheltered. At the end she turns left down Marchfield Road into the face of the wind again. Here she can see the Tay River which she recognises as the source of the watery and salty scent even if she doesn't completely understand what it is. She makes a right into Grosvenor Road. At the tall stone cemetery wall the road ends and to the left a narrow lane runs down to Perth Road. Minnie doesn't take the lane. She hops through the grill of a gate to the right and trots up a driveway before clambering through a gap in the hedge that leads into a gap in the fenced part of the cemetery boundary.

She is in. She scans the terrain. Not even a bird stirs. Her bladder is throbbing and she hurriedly finds her favourite spot behind a tall thin gravestone of reddish hue.

Feeling relieved and calmer she begins to cover the hole when a strange sensation passes over her. It is as though she can feel the presence of another being. A human. She looks around and sees nothing. Suddenly it is upon her and she is caught. She still can't see anything but she feels it coming into her body and wrenching it from her.

Minnie freezes mid step. Her mouth opens and

closes but no noise comes out. {Wait! Can it be? Yes! I'm in! I'm in! I'm back! Hahahaha! Alive! I can't believe it. Out of the dirt. Hahaha. Whooooo! Out of the muddy traces of my remains! Away from the worms and the sludge. The endless darkness and nothingness. I am substance! I am real! I can taste the fresh air. And my oh my! What strong sight and hearing and smell I have. Maybe a cat wasn't such a bad host after all! I wasted far too many years trying to enter those miserable mourners. Speaking of miserable. Best of all about being up here is being away from those miserable fuddy-duddies down there! Oh the decades of having to listen to their dreary monologues. Constantly reminding me of why I left Dundee in the first place. Hahaha! Those fools said it couldn't be done. They said wait it out. They claimed that only when the last remnants of an earthly body turned to dirt could the soul ascend. Oh yes? And how would they know? Old Gemma, the first person buried in the cemetery is still around after nearly two centuries! So posh posh to their nonsense. Hahaha! I can just picture it. They'll be wondering where I've gone. Where's Tom? What do you mean? He's not here. Come now. No, I mean it. What's going on? I have no idea. Weren't you just talking to him? I was. I was telling him about my favourite Boxing Day meals. He said his was cold pudding with peace and quiet. Then we both noticed the cat. He complained that it always went for his grave. And then nothing. Complete silence. It's most strange. Where could he be? Let's ask Catherine. Catherine? What? Where's Tom? Where we all are. Nowhere. Dead. No Catherine we're serious we can't sense him at all. Hmmm neither can I now that you mention it. How peculiar. What does it mean? He's left us! No! Impossible! Preposterous! Etc, etc. Hahahaha! Those imbeciles! The only thing that could entice me back would be the pleasure of hearing their silly confusion. But now... More pressing matters. No time to lose. Where to? Golly I hadn't thought this far ahead. Think… think… You're a cat. Let's start by seeing what this cat can do.} Her front left paw lifts and lowers several times. {Hmm not bad. It's a start. Quite a lot of effort though. I expect it'll get easier. Ok let's try the other.} The right does the same. {And let's finish with the back two.} Then each hind leg. {Good, good. I think I'm getting it. Let's try some full body movement.} She treads forward with an odd and stilted step. {Here we go. Now we're talking. Yippee! One step two step three step four step one step two step… I'll be out of here in no time!}

For no apparent reason she stops and releases a distressed yowl. {Wait! What the devil was that? I didn't do that! Oh I can feel it now. I'm not alone. The animal is in here with me. What abhorrent presence! So primal! We're vying for supremacy. This will be harder than I thought. But nothing is easy. It wants to rid itself of me. I must swell up. I must dominate. Take the little beast by the reins. Aaarrrghh! Aaaaarrghh!) Several spasms shake her body and she falls flat to the ground. {Baaaah! Gggaaaah! Back beast! Back I say! This body is mine! Raaaaarr! Raaaarrr! Gggggggggggggggggah!} No sooner has she fallen than she recovers and stands again. {Whew! There we are. I think I have it. But it's not completely gone. It lurks, clinging on. Now I know what I must do. I must find an empty vessel. Yes. The mourners have often spoken of the university mortuary. I will find a body there. A human body in need of a human soul. Time to leave this accursed cemetery! Ah! This is much easier going with the animal subdued. I could get used to this! Great nimble agility!} With a spritely step she crosses several plots to reach the central path and trots down its incline. For one brief instant she appears to flinch or even grimace but she doesn't stop. {Oh! Down below! Curses. There it is. That dreadful river. How ghastly! Why would my parents bury me within sight of my murderer? It beggars belief. Bad enough it unceasingly haunts me ever since that fateful night. So long ago. Yet so vivid. I was so naïve! And arrogant. There I was. Sitting on the train. Content as could be. Not a fear in the world. On my long overdue visit home from

London. I'd spent the previous night in Edinburgh visiting my old law Professor. Gaily reporting on my professional success down south. One night in my homeland had increased my impatience to see my parents after so many years. I was even more excited to break the news of my engagement. They'd almost given up on the possibility. I could already picture their shocked, happy faces. No nothing could dampen my mood. Not even the tumultuous ferry crossing at Forth and the increasingly ghastly wind over Fife. By the time we reached the Tay Bridge the tempest was at its most ferocious. So conceited was I that I almost laughed at the nervousness of my fellow passengers. I heard one say to another, If it's safe enough for Queen Victoria it's safe enough for us. What about me? I thought. I'm one of Dundee's finest! Risen to the top of the legal profession in London and on an overdue homecoming with gay tidings for proud parents. No storm can stop me! ... I seriously thought this. Even as we mounted the bridge and felt the full force of the wind tilting the train. Even as the sparks came off the wheels grinding against the rail. Even as the locomotive groaned and the women and children screamed. Even as the men joined in the screams. It was only when I heard and felt the greater structure break below me that I realised the peril. There the weighty drop I can still feel within me. The darkness.

The thud. The cold water rising. The yearning for air. And then nothing...} The main entrance gate is closed. {Oh! Dear me! Mustn't dwell on the past! A new opportunity in my grasp! An adventure! Tally-ho! Lord knows where it will end. Perhaps nowhere. So enjoy it while you can my dear fellow. Anywhere is better than down there. It's not the destination it's the journey and all that. But firstly how to get out of here?} Minnie turns along the entrance wall and finds a side gate with wide grills a metre up from the ground. {Aha! A perfect challenge. Let's try this. Whoop!} Without breaking stride she leaps through and out onto the pavement below. {Lovely! Such light grace in this body. Hm. I know where we are. It's coming back. My hometown beckons.} She heads west along Perth Road. {I can feel my senses honing too. They're already far beyond anything I remember. All thanks to this feline form. It is cold. The town is quiet. I can smell the Tay and some wood fires. I can taste rich food. Ah yes! It's Boxing Day. Are these the objects the mourners refer to as cars? Bah! There'll be plenty of time to get acquainted with novelties later. I must hurry. I can feel the restless animal. It's making me nervous. I mustn't flinch. Focus. Focus on being one with the body. Hark! Someone on the footpath. I must get off Perth Road. Stick to the side roads. Up here.} At the approach of a lone pedestrian she turns up Grosvenor Road and onto

Shaftesbury Lane.

Minnie breaks into a fast canter. {Let's speed it up a bit. The energy and sprite of this creature is tremendous! Front limbs back limbs front limbs back limbs. Dadumpdadumpdadump. What enchanting rhythm. Divine swiftness. I'll be at the mortuary in no time! I might come to miss this vehicle.} Three houses ahead a large tomcat sitting on a low stone wall beside a hedge spies her coming and crouches. As Minnie passes he lunges with his claws and fangs brandished. {Whoa! What in God's name was that! Scared the devil out of me!} Minnie tumbles and after a second of lying limp she drags herself up and faces her nemesis. {Another cat! With an evil look. Out for some violence I dare say.} The tomcat arches his back and stares her down. {A duel my good sir? Alright you sod. Prepare for a lesson you won't forget. You don't know who you're dealing with. I'm not your average cat. I was champion boxer at university! And I have passed through death! I am a feline Lazarus! Meet your maker!} Minnie doesn't hiss or yowl. She clumsily strikes out with both her paws. {Take that you fiend! Got him! And that and that! Stop moving you coward!} Her first swipe scratches the tomcat's nose but he easily avoids her other attempts. He darts to her side and launches upon her. {Ah he is quick! Where is he?} His claws dig in as he grips her body. {Aaarrgh! What agony!

He is on me! I can feel his weight. Every one of his nails digging into my hide! Ever tighter! What is this at my neck! No no no no no! Get off!} He plunges his teeth into her throat. {Owww! Damn this useless body! Fight! Get off! Ah! The agony! Graah! Yes! There! I can breathe! I...} Minnie squirms and momentarily frees her neck only for the tomcat to dig his claws in tighter and bring his fangs down on a more precarious location. {Aaaaaaaaah! Curse those little daggers! No! Not his fangs again! Not there! Be gone you brute! Isn't one death enough for me? What will happen if... it happens again? I can't let it. Fight! Focus! Muster every ounce of strength. But wait... What's happening? No! The animal within is making its move! Stop! Back beast! It sees opportunity in my predicament. Back! Back I say! Nooooo! They have me. They're smothering me from outside and within. I fear the worst! Who will mourn me this time? No! I mustn't think about the funeral. I mustn't think of heartbreak more painful than dying. It's too overwhelming and I mustn't be distracted... But where was she? Why didn't she attend my funeral? And why did she not once visit my grave? It's too much to bear. Did she never truly love me? Now she is dead. Like me. Why bother. What use is life to someone who was never truly loved? Ooohooh! Why am I thinking this now? In this grave moment! Or is it only fitting that this memory of devastation should seal my fate… So be it! I have lost all resolve. I am slipping… Wait! No! I mustn't let go! I must fight! No! It's too late! I'm slipping! I can't hold on! … I…}

Suddenly Minnie launches herself backwards and crashes down on the tomcat. She lets out an enormous screech and pulls free. In an instant she is facing the tomcat and hissing and lashing. She pierces and tears his ear and he senses the first premonition of defeat. A claw narrowly misses his eye. As he backs away she catches his tail and feels the flesh shred as he pulls free. He jumps over the wall and is gone.

Minnie doesn't give chase. She licks several of the bleeding wounds in her side before it occurs to her to seek the safety of home.

She hurries down Hyndford Street and across Blackness Avenue. At Blackness Road she briefly glances each way and scampers to the other side. She joins Max sitting on the outside window ledge staring in. Minnie meows and scratches the pane.

Ahyrit ahyrit, comes a voice from inside. The window opens and Minnie and Max hurry through the gap. Minnie's owner doesn't notice the bleeding wounds masked amongst her black fur. Minnie rushes to the food bowl and finds some turkey bones to tussle over with Max. She spends the best part of the evening washing and nursing herself.

Cheryl McGregor

Peter Street, Late Evening

the wind picks up east-beasts
and lets them loose on every corner
they howl in ears,
      down the backs of necks,
            as they dogtrot their way
                  down the street.

the streetlight wears the crown o' nazareth
upon its luminous head
it coruscates the cobbled lane
where the living ghosts emerge

they side-step
      shuffle their way
down the street.

Laura Strathern

Quiddity

The beetles have already eaten half the cheese.
I threw the candles out the window. Two of them
     were still lit, but nothing exploded. I don't know
     why I expected some Molotov cocktail effect.
The half of the cheese that's left is not really edible
     anymore.
Kirsty is swimming at Carnoustie beach and is not
     replying to my texts.
I don't even like phones. I hope mine explodes.
What are beetles supposed to eat, even?
That camembert wasn't cheap you know…
Update – They don't care.
My front step smells like cinnamon now. Because
     of the wax everywhere I guess. At least nothing
     caught fire, except the honeysuckle.
The honeysuckle was actually my favourite.
I'm going to go out, and buy candles of all different
     flavours, everything except cinnamon.
I'm going to go out and buy no candles, because
     actually I hate candles, they give me a headache.
I'm going to go out and buy a honeysuckle bush.
– Maybe even two.
The beetles are asleep when I get back.
It turns out I don't know how to plant things. The
     honeysuckles are going to be indoor plants for a
     while.

I think the beetles might have died, they haven't
  moved all day.

I've watched *The Mummy* too many times to trust
  them, but I do feel a bit guilty, maybe they're
  lactose intolerant?

Kirsty called. She says she is now hang-gliding in
  Kinnesswood, can I keep the beetles for another
  night. Under the circumstances, I don't object.

At least I can eat this cheddar in peace. All the
  pieces.

Oh, no – the beetles were just playing possum. My
  new honeysuckles have beetle bites out of them.

I am not a beetle babysitter. I am putting my foot
  down.

I could go hang-gliding if I wanted. Sometimes fear
  is a choice.

A very rational, sane choice. Kirsty is now in
  hospital with a broken wrist.

I wonder if beetles know what possums are.

Tesco does not sell beetle food. Or possums.

Kirsty texted "Hang-gliding was great fun, I'm
  going sky diving next week."

Thanks for the invite.

"You would totally wet yourself."

Whatever.

She said she broke her wrist not from the stupid
  death inducing sports but from punching a man
  in the face. That's so much better.

I take the beetles on the train with me. Not just all
    roaming around obviously, they're in their box-
    tank thing. I show them the new train station,
    looking snazzy. I think they were really excited
    by that.

I think the conductor was not really excited by
    them.

I glare at her because, there's nothing wrong with
    my beetles, or with people who take beetles on
    trains.

We are heading through to Arbroath and we are
    having our own adventure.

Kirsty calls and I can smell cinnamon through the
    phone. Am I having a stroke, or am I just an
    idiot?

She says she is in the flat. She says I am not there
    and neither are the beetles. Well I already knew
    that, duh, I am rolling my eyes at her a lot right
    now.

I tell her I have named the beetles Paul and
    McCartney and John and Lennon and Yellow
    Submarine because I can't remember the names
    of the other Beatles, if there really were more
    than two.

Kirsty gets a bit cross and says how uninventive that
    is.

I am the daughter of two accountants, I am not
    supposed to be inventive, I am supposed to be

clever and sensible. She says I am not that either.
I really set her up for that one.

I take Paul, McCartney, John, Lennon, and Yellow
to the chippie by the harbour.

I tell them, this might be even better than cheese.

Kirsty says I am no longer a beetle baby-sitter but a
beetle baby-napper.

I say who is she, Doctor Seuss?

She knows I am weak for Doctor Seuss.

I tell her she can always pop down on the train and
meet us, it is only twenty minutes. She says yes,
she will do that.

I feed Paul and John and the gang some of my fish
and chips, but I'm not sure they agree with the
cheese comparison.

They are cute, really, once you get past how creepy
and ugly they are.

Kirsty opens the cage-box-tank and kisses them
each one by one.

I saved her some of my chips.

I share chips with almost no one.

I think she appreciates my romantic gesture because
she smiles and starts calling the beetles by their
Beatles names. She gets Lennon mixed up with
Paul but I don't point this out right now.

We hold hands and walk along the cliffs.

I hold the gang in their box in my other hand
because Kirsty's wrist is broken and a bit sore.

We cuddle up out of the wind, picking at chips
   with cold fingers, and watch the sun setting over
   the harbour.
Kirsty says "This might be even better than hang–
   gliding" and kisses my cheek.
I say "I'm sorry I threw all your candles out the
   window".
Kirsty says "What?"

Reece Robertson

Where I'm From

A burst of colour and music and venetian-style revelry possess my senses, and I know that I have arrived. Worlds within worlds, I feel like I've been let into some strange pocket of reality – where everyone is decked out in alien garb and speaking in accents far too pronounced and proper for me to consider opening my own mouth (lest I let them know that I don't belong). People wearing neon masks with warping, patterned tuxedos are huddled gracefully in a corner, playing some old music that is an objective kind of beautiful. There are a myriad of scents and flavours which impossibly occupy exact spaces in this grand foyer. The smell of fruit, meats, perfumes, homemade bread, and flowers ever so lightly brush you as you move along. As I make my way into the main ballroom I am running my tongue across my teeth, sucking at the spaces inbetween as if I've just taken a satisfying bite from an apple. It's a clean, sharp taste and the recreation is so effective, that I get the slightest inclination my gums have started bleeding.

The doors that lead into the ballroom are dwarfing, and over the swathe of decorative headpieces which adorn the people at home at such an event as this, I spy to my amazement legs and shoes dangling from the exceedingly high, high ceiling. These legs, which I can see now are attached to dancing bodies, are clad in all white. They laugh and giggle, but from so far below, I only hear the faintest traces of their voices. They drift slowly and with weight, as if underwater. There are just a few of them up there, tumbling gracefully, throwing each other around – and they distract me passionately from the dancing bombast, the traditional ballroom happenings about me on this level. I'm down here, but I want to be up there.

"Beautiful, aren't they?"

I turn to find a tall woman, dressed in the same kind of otherworldly attire as the rest of the patrons, hers red in colour, staring at me through a fluffy mask that seems half-alive. She's smiling.

"How are they doing that?"

She smiles wider.

"Magic. I'm going to assume this is your first time at the Montpellier?"

"Is it that obvious?"

"It's sweet, the new folk have a way of making this place feel special again."

"You're telling me this isn't special to you anymore?"

"If you stick around long enough cherub, then it will all lose its charm eventually. Breathtaking otherwise. For people like you, I mean."

People like you.

"I bet you haven't seen the wall yet", she adds, a sudden energy in her voice.

"The wall?"

The Woman nods her head softly and gestures to a spot upstairs. The rabble of the ballroom, its spark and party, going on as normal beneath her extended arm.

"I'll show you" she says, and with no warning turns and walks away, melting into the bright crowd of impeccable fabrics and particular cadences – expecting, and knowing, that I will dutifully follow.

I catch up with her on the stairs. The bannister here is made of some strong glass, that bends and distorts the ballroom lights in such a way as to project tiny rainbow arches in its detail.

"That's a funny little accent you have there, Scottish isn't it?"

"That's right."

The Woman's decorated leg stretches through the threshold at the end of the staircase and into a warmly lit hallway. A far cry from the bright visage of the ballroom – this space is decidedly dark. Low lit, with walls coloured a deep red, velvet in texture. Even the sound changes, the laughter and the music of the ballroom sharply turning to mumble as we press onward. My hand instinctively reaches out to brush the rich texture of the red wall. The fingers sink in. It's so warm. I might just sink in too.

"Where in Scotland are you from, cherub?"

"Dundee", I pull away from the wall.

"I think I may have been there" she says, "or near it anyway. Anywhere in particular?"

"A place called Whitfield."

"Never heard of it."

"You wouldn't have. It's a scheme...a housing estate."

Her red mask twitches just a touch, and in the dark cast of the mask's eyeholes I can see a twinge of interest.

"Just what are you doing here then?"

She doesn't let me answer.

"Tell me more about Whitfield. I'm interested."

"I don't know what there is to say. It's where I'm from, that's kind of it. There's nothing there y'know? Like, nothing."

"There can't be nothing, think harder cherub".

I try.

"It's rough, y'know? Or it used to be. Like any other scheme I guess. I'm not even sure anymore to tell the truth, it's been a while since I was there."

"Down here."

We've reached the end of the hall, and as I look up to find the Woman I spy just the tail-end of her glitter-soaked dress fluttering downward and out of sight through a second staircase. It's even darker down there, with only the dim light from the bottom allowing us to see anything – and all that I can, is her flowery and tall silhouette, beckoning me with a finger to follow.

I do.

A wide, open space – dark – with a small number of doors leading to who knows what part of this strange estate. I don't think about that, I focus on the wall. The Woman stands a little off to my side as I approach it, my face illuminated with each step and my vision swarmed with a shining display of bonnie nature. Flowers, plants and growth of all colours decorate this wall, interweaving in high decoration. Defying gravity, there is a thick stream of water that runs through the centre – flowing from the bottom up, sparkling and clean. Butterflies and hummingbirds flutter above as I reach out and press my palm onto the soft grass. So close to it now, the source-less light grows warmer, and for a moment I close my eyes, I forget that I'm in some midnight mansion. I could stay here forever, like someone painted their wall with a summer's day.

"This is amazing."

"I bet you don't see this kind of thing back in Whitfield."

"How is something like this even possible? How is any of it possible?"

The Woman just smiles and glides over to the Wall. With a gloved finger she gently traces alongside the backwards stream, running it down all the way from as far as her long arms can reach, to a resting cluster of red and white spotted mushrooms.

"Try one?" she asks, plucking two with a satisfying 'pop'.

I hesitate.

"I don't know. They're magic right?"

"Everything is."

She holds one out to me and nods, encouraging.

The red colour is so stark that it looks unreal, with all of the aesthetic property and draw of a sugar-rich, fruity sweet. Taking it between my fingers, I turn my attention back to the Woman. No ceremony, she throws the other mushroom into her mouth and begins to chew – and with that, I follow.

It tastes of nothing.

"Should we go back to the party?"

"No. Not yet. We should play first."

"Play?"

"Yes, play. There's plenty of time to dance, and there's more of this place I want to show you first."

I don't get much time to think before she begins spinning me around, whirring and wooing as if playing with a child. This close to her now, towering over me, I feel like one. But I don't protest. I don't resist. I find myself facing the wall when she stops me, and then she commands:

"Count to twenty, then come find me."

"But – "

"No cherub, just do as I say. Twenty seconds."

I can hear the Woman's clicking footsteps grow fainter as the bright of the wall holds me still. Soon, I hear nothing – and when I realise that I am alone in this place, a rush of panic takes its grip. A palpable and visceral fear. I don't count to twenty, instead I turn to face the empty room, and with heavy breath search for the exit. Part of me wants to just turn around and engage with the Wall again – discerning each kind of flower, taking in the myriad summer aromas until the Woman or someone else comes along to find me, but I'm beginning to sweat.

Each step is spitting echoes through this dark space, and I can feel the warm light of the Wall fall gradually from my back. There is a sudden creep to everything. The staircase from before offers some light relief, the inviting light at its tip encouraging me to scurry onwards, until I slip on one of the steps. The red walls, they're so much less inviting than before, the entire hallway feels off. I struggle to swallow, my throat itchy and dry. I reach out my hand to touch the velvet wall – awaiting the comfortable sensation I had felt before – but instead, it feels like moss. Damp. I rip my hand away in disgust, and I find that my palms are sweating profusely. There is a different kind of sinking in my chest, as I recognise I have been standing here for a long time.

"Oh god".

I need to leave.

There is a thumping in the floor and in the newly repulsive walls, a rhythmic and heavy music. I follow the sound and hope it will lead me back to the ballroom. There I can stumble nervously through the fancy dancers, take one last look at the floating people in their white suits and then make my escape. Instead, I find myself opening doors to an expansive and peopled lounge area decorated with red wood walls and eerie taxidermy, like some old forest lodge. Each of my senses buzzes with input, clawing for my attention as the atmosphere about me so dramatically shifts – from a cold, quiet anxiety into a roaring, hot one. The room is pulsing on every level. From the music, which is low and throbbing – its tones dragging across the floor and everything else, to the people; who are braying and dancing from the back of their throats. The heat too is immense, radiating from a fire-place the size of a whole wall. The people are scattered around the place, with some just talking, some throwing themselves around and others, most strangely, marching in time to the music that cuts right through me. Their faces are devoid of any expression, following one another in a circle – half naked and slippery.

Despite the great heat I start to shiver, and so hold my arms tight as I walk further into the room. The noise, temperature and smell are making me ill but I push on, trying to find someone – the Woman –

who might help me get out of here. All these people seem sick. Their masks and costumes are slipping with the sweat – and it's giving away their ugliness. The mushroom is working fast on me, as the faces begin to warp and twist in a nightmarish fashion. I'm crumbling. My knees are shaky, and they are all laughing, so I start running as fast as I can. Bodies and furniture crash into me at every turn, every mask and costume turning sinister – but I don't stop until I reach the exit. I am dripping now, and I struggle to close the door behind me.

I slump against the wall before I hear a familiar laughter hanging along the banister of a new staircase. Moving to its first step and looking up, the spiral feels like it will suck me in. It takes me a moment to notice her. The Woman, leaning over, looking down on me. She's waving, and I run to her. She turns this to chase, and soon I find myself sprinting around and up, with the Woman always a few inches ahead of me. The staircase moves with us, a cartoonish conveyer belt that sprint fast, keeping us in stasis. The speed is too much. I think I will die on fire before I find myself flung to the top of the staircase. Everything is buzzing and I am on my knees. A welcomed sense of slow washes over me, and I take a second to enjoy before I notice that the Woman has vanished again. I try to stand still, but wobble and feel the sensation of great height in this new space.

I can hear her laughing on the other side of the door ahead of me, and my heart sinks. Her laughing is affected in some way. Sounds off. I fight the urge to sob as I realise something is very wrong. I open the door, and the Woman is flailing in the air. Clawing at the high ceiling with blood gargling out of her. She's crying, retching, and laughing – it's now clear to me that this is the effect of some sort of drug. A drug only the wealthiest can get their hands on. Her red mask has fallen off, and I can see the real person underneath it. Her eyes are so wide they look like they might fall out, her skin stretches far and wide as she giggles uncontrollably.

I am overwhelmed, and although I am aware this may be some sort of hallucination, something throws me forward into a jump – stretching out my hands in an attempt to grab hold of her. The ceiling is too tall, and each emphatic leap takes more out of me. I don't stop. She keeps laughing. Using all my strength, I try once more but fall harshly onto my ribs.

"Help!" I shout. Begging that someone will hear me, "Help!"

With one sharp intake of breath she finally stops. There is a quiet moment, as she falls silent. The Woman's body is still floating, but begins to aimlessly bump against the roof, drifting along.

"Help, please! Please! Somebody help me!"

My throat is tearing with the screams. My hands

are gripping my head, nails digging into my scalp as I try to break the moment.

Nobody comes.

I drag myself through to the bedroom next door. There are tall, clear windows which give way to the courtyard. The remaining ballroomers are clinking champagne glasses and hurrahing far below me, as terrific fireworks dominate the sky. As I look at the display I am suddenly struck with a memory. A group of neds, throwing fireworks – launching them into a crowd of us outside Braeview as we headed home. I'm fifteen. We ran, and I took refuge in an old, abandoned house.

I sit on a wide, grand poster-bed and I wish it was less comfortable. I lie down and wish that I could hear the noisy air-conditioning that hums from the back of the shops directly across the street from my bedroom. They're finding her now. I wish I could hear a group of kids kicking a bin over and laughing. I'm falling asleep. I want to hate where I'm from again, be embarrassed by it, bored of it – but now I understand how things really are. I can hear someone shouting from across the hall. I wish I was in Whitfield.

I wish I was at home.

Zan de Parry

DUNDEE DAY

they say something hit you
in the head younger
put it in lord mode but I don't know why I stopped

three-to-four standing paddlers
and I think it's you there
hard-balancing that rocking Tay

imagining me / that
ankles my legs
gets me in the presence

here's where I'll be: Dundee

DUNDEE NIGHT

the veins of my chest turned up
as a blue spectacle of hands covering each other

soap was yellow still on you
grown-up date flavor
the night kept saying a glowing *us*, shall we say

us! can you hear it?
the babe singing *mama*
in his papa's arms?
the beat
of his little detail???

W.N. Herbert

Address to the Dundee V n A

Bilbao, Paree, Thatlondon, thon Hull
o aa the braa toons that tourists could visit
why pick on Dundee? It's duller than Mull
and the hame o the Broons – plus, whaur the hell
is it?
Pit a daud o V n A in wir DNA
and let's see whit Dundee can dae.
(And gee the Laa Hull monument a Prince Albert
beh the way.)

Zenimalism for the zenimals!
Lemonalism for the Jif Lemon Tree!
Municipalism fur wir new principles!
Hing-em-fae-a-lampie-ism fur the auld kleptocracy!

Let's hae a kulchural kouplet, tae prove we're no aa
zoomers:
skate like a Pingu, strike like a puma
build the V n A like a Kengo Kuma…
Geez anither, fur Eh feel we grow less snidey:
the V n A is lookin tidy
lit by nicht like a silver bridie.

Hi ho, drinkers in the Waalnut Lounge, or ye
wha in Mennie's snack on nosh
wi mebbe a wee OVD n coke:

why no inhale a siller bridie or
a plenn ane wi a whack of squash
inna tearoom that's no only bespoke
but pretty V n A n oke?
Then spend yir penny backin Scotch
design beh Rennie Mackintosh!

Let's hear whit we'd clamour fur inna Wunderkammer
–
Somethin mair nor the history o the peh
via an incredible edible Land o Cakes visit it n-deh-
orama!

Eh'd want tae ken fae Kengo, micht it be whit we
craw 'humour'
or is there any truth tae the scurrilous rumour
(be it wondrous story or spurious conjecture)
that, deep in noo-borassic laboratories,
the V n A is growein back the architecture
o demolished Victorian and Albertine Dundee?

See, were it up tae me, or in meh gift,
a new Auld Wellgate and Overgate wad descend fae
the lift,
also a new spire fur the Royal Excheenge weavit
softsift
frae thon maist precious metal, Nostalgium,
signifehin that the Kengo-dom o Kuma hud indeed

come –
basically a new spine fur Dei Donum
biggit fae seevin whale vertebrae sellt affa barra
threidit thru wi the sangs o Brooksbank and o Marra
lyk therr wiz literally nae thimorra.

Gee us a museum that's no jist a mirror but a witness
tae the toun o whale ile, liberty, and sweetness,
tae uts lairdies and uts cairdies that noo are wede
away,
let the canny and uncanny deid speak within oor V
n A.

27th Doldrum

Fellini fiss oan thi Nummer 73
mune-broch o dehed black herr aroond
yir perfickly medd-upness, fictive Signora o
    thi late fifties tae early seeventies,
bus-pass fae thi Ferry that beh
thi Liz Taylored arc o yir broo
        shid tak ye tae thi Grand Canal
   or at least thi Dorsoduro, curvin lyk yir spine,
thi bus a vaporetto noo, sliderin
   thru thi decades past
 thi Eastern Necropolis, Diaghilev and Ezra therein,
mascara *maschera* fur thi wintry
festa della nonna in Piazza Santa Margherita,
 an Aperol or an Irn Bru afore ye,
fluttirbeh shades i thi thinnin sun,
                  Peggy Glugginhame
 doon thi Strips o Craigie and up
      past the *palazzos di iuta*, mooth
a Montalcino o lippie, a Loren-lie calligraphy
    o thi unsaid, thi lang untelt,
      thi nivir-comin hame...

28th Doldrum (The Fireman's Daughter)

Staunin in Broon Street fissin a waa, fissin awa
frae whaur thi Fire Station wiz, and aside ut,
thi hoose o thi heid fireman, and in ut,
        thi heid fireman's dochter.
This bein thi semm sad sandstane waa,
grey unyieldin strips, that wiz
oor vertical mattress: pressin ilk intae ither oan ut,
een
tae een,
            mooth oan mooth,
                        breist tae breist –
ivrythin o us on ocht but whit wiz ahent me:
hame's doonhaudin wecht.
                        Aa oor lorn subornin
a future owre faur aff that shairly wid
but didnae come.
                    Turn and aa's dung doon,
hoose and station, dochter and iver
meetin in this life: the meenut wiz
thi life, timed oot, thi kiss thi mairriage, unbeddit.
Turn and aa's brunt
                    i thi years' ships' bombardment. Turn
and Editor Doldrum shows thi cut – no even
thi fuss o sma toun Eurydice fadin intae
hir ackshully be'er life
  lyk the dauphin's fin i thi Tay –

aa's gane, aa's tint, aa's slaw
    sleight: wiz this yir caird? Naw.
        Wiz this? Naw, that wiznae ut.

Ode to Yit Anither Dundee Railway Station

O beautiful new Dundee Railway Station
for which they should have added, as Ringo advises,
an eighth day to Creation,
tho who 'they' are is akin to a knotty theological
question
concerning the 'sons of God'★, which rather
lies outside the frame of the famous sticksman's
suggestion
-unless it's the Etruscans, who passed an eight day
week on
to the Romans, granting them just that little longer
to get thir freak on –
something Dun-loving-fundonians micht appreciate
mair than you,
ye big bendy gless banana descendit on us as thi tae
spite the EU.
For like the bairns o thae sons of God wha ligged wi
the dochters of men
ye're neither hake nor drake, nor are you but nor
ben.
Hauf-chuff chuff station an hauf yit anither bluidy
hotel
fur the prayed-fur kulchur rush – tho this wan
cannae spell –
fae 'Sleeperz' tae the V n A,
tho but a pace, is a demographic league away.

And you are less lovely, let's face it,

than the splendid Italianate then Gothic constructions
yir shabby predecessor replaceit.

For if there's one thing Dundee Cooncil likes mair
than a guid deal

it's a deal that lets them knoack doon historic
buildings as weel.

But of this as of aesthetic style you are wholly
unkennan

the way that folk don't really know who the best
drummer in the Beatles wiz, according to John
Lennon★

, or God or the Etruscans or the need for
Renationalisation –

who cares while there's a crap hotel humping
Dundee Station?

★(Genesis 6: 1-4)
★ Actually attributed to Jasper Carrot

Address to the Girders

O beautiful railway girders, which bridge the still
Victorian Tay,
so strong and broad and even:
who could have prophesied you would inspire one
day
Irn Bru Yum Yums for sale in Goodfellow & Steven's?
A bakey orange marvel of the present day,
Which for just 95p in new money can be taken
away!

O girders, which so beautifully bridge the unrustable
Tay
How I wish you delivered teapots to McGonagall
each day,
Teapots the size of bathtubs wherein he could disport
and play
with the whalefish and the seal-people and the
spratlings of the Tay,
and serve them and me Spicy Red Chai from
Braithewaite's changeless urns
and thae Yum Yums for which even drooned fowks
yearns!

Though gradually wir flesh would tak on the colour
o Trumpo or United

and wir teeth dissolved tae bridge stumps, still, aa
wad be delighted!

29th Doldrum (Snugs)

Lament fur the snugz o thi Ferry,
made tartan corridors fur thi insertion
   o deep-frehd camemberts intae thi baald
and thir wifies, wha cannae help thirsels fae
glaik-goyin at thi gowk
                           caucht at his dirty drinkin –
Eh, moi, masel, wi nae taste fur yir widescreen
      fitbaw inferno: eternal wee legs o sinners
   denehd
aa hope o Heivin beh thi Auld Firm's ticht
   heuristics.

Thi snell wund blaas thru shoogly swing doors
whaur, thirty years back, we ghaist bairns sat
at thi ghaists o tables, pressin ghaist buttons fur
pints o MacGhaist's, thi nicht thick an bleezin
      wi tales o thae futures we niver did see.

Lament fur yir kneebanes, waarm as stanes
   oan a beach, awaitin Demosthenes Megalostoma;
lament fur yir dwaums o snugs braw as banvas,
      Soutar-and-Shanterin wi thi wick an flicker
   o coals,
holy as thi tongues o sanctit gowks we niver gote
   tae be
but beh default,

caucht oot beh
                    thi turnin tide,
Tay's neist indifference aye takkin us beh
        thi semm, jaa-hingin, mum surprehz.

30th Doldrum (Cloud City)

They didnae even let them collect aa thae
         white letters aff the frunt o Halleys
                afore they dung ut doon –
sae aff the auld jutemill tuke, hauf-nemmless
        as tho intae air or ether, but insteid ut wiz
    thi either
    side o or, as in 'ye cuid knock ut doon, or...',
but this is Dingutdoondee, sae Halley's awa
        intae the nithin atween Dundonian stars,
comet wove o frore memory, anely tae retour
  i thi wee resurrection o photies, or prophetic
    thocht
whaurin thi hail toon sall be rebiggit
        at the pole or oan thi Mune
whichever micht occur least sune:

  Nephelolithogenethlialocheeakokkygia
weavit fae *altocumulonumbnuts nonmutatisdundi*
    cloods
beh mithers themsels medd o hauf reid herrins'
    banes
    and hauf noddin horsehair plumes and ponytails
tae snare and terrifeh ony Vicarious Nastyanax
    as cares tae tumble beh.

When uts exiled dwaums bigg mair o a toon
nor its cooncillors' schemes can ding doon
makkin Alexandrian a herbour that's nae mair
nor a pelvis o sandstane; recoverin AntiRhodos fae
the thrapple o Tay; swirlin and birlan the Wellgate
    i thi swellachie o thi Ladywell till
Mannahatta is medd o thi Hulltoon,
and a cathedral fur Logie and Erasmian colleges
    ur foondit whaur the Ice Rink wiz demolished.

    Thi 45 cinemas sall be refurbished,
    aa departments restored in Draffens,
D.M. Browns, Robertsons, McGills lit beh nicht
    till Blackness is rebiggit –
    meh skail as memory palace fur thi dole proles:
buiks flap lyk ainguls i thi steep storm o sleepin air
    whaur uts classrooms wull sit.

    Nithin in Dundee can be destroyit eftir aa
nor can ut be deTroyit since ilka mind here and
awa
hauds ut, minds ut,
                    city upon city, nicht beh nicht,
                                        dwaums ut,
haunnin ut oan lyk a tuneless ballat, or very like
    ane epic
  meh hametoon's Homers'll tell ye whaur
the Pola-Cola Bear noo set amang thi stars

wiz furst penntit oanna wwaa; whaur Glebe Street
stude
    back when Paw Broon wiz a young Stobie boy
that syne is Auchenshooglet awa;
                            they'll recite
the genealogy o ivry chipper lyk a lost ship list.

Sue Haigh

V and A

On Friday 14th September 2018, members of four Dundee-based community choirs under the musical directorship of Alice Marra, sang the Deacon Blue song, Dignity, at the opening preview of the new V&A Museum of Design in Dundee. The following piece reflects the experiences of choir members on the night.

"*We had a wonderful time working on the arrangement of Dignity. It was a fantastic way of getting so many Dundonians involved in the opening of the building and it was extremely emotional to watch 150 of them belt out the song in such fabulous surroundings.*"
Alice Marra, Musical Director

Opening night of the new V&A! Alice said,
Once in a lifetime experience,
our privilege to sing on a global stage.
Momentous, historic occasion –
Almost overwhelming to start.
Jings, crivvens, help ma boab!

Stunning iconic building,
famous from here to Montreal.
Outside – angular, mysterious, grey;
chasm inside – welcoming and warm,

inspiring Dundonians new and old;
monument to the silvery Tay.

Smuggled in, hushed and huddled,
hidden from view, one hundred and fifty strong,
secret choir in the ante-room.
Waiting to surprise with a
proud anthem by one of our own;
Dignity in Dundee.

Nerve-wracked, excited, butterflies
Emotional with hope of
A bright future for my city.
Ahffae reilehsation, stannin there, waihin,
Wir ii cappella cwhiiur,
Nae insrimints tae help us oot, jist oor voices!

Steely blue, a river flowing
starting small, confidence growing,
filling the cavernous space. Vast
Voices swirling up to the gallery
creating magic between
the city's future and her past.

Breathtaking cheering, whistling, clapping;
gave me goosebumps, like something snapping.
Greeting like wee lassies, bursting with pride.
Eh wus convinced when eh opened meh mooth

nae soohnd whud come oot.
Bhu Dignity didni lih iz doon.

Aspirations of the council worker;
of all who toil thanklessly
for the dream of a better way of living
reflect our ambitions
for this amazing, creative city.
Singing, staking our claim, we are Dundee.

It was my birthday, it was fun,
wouldn't have missed it for the world.
Proud of the impressive sound;
our choir, our collaboration, our community.
Returning belief in my creative abilities –
Strong bonds and Dignity empowering me.

Moments in rehearsal ever etched;
shared aim, relationships strengthened.
Cunnehktin wie ane in ither, behin whaurr
Ane boadie, three perts, catched in time
Oor ancesturs whur aah here inah
Timeless experiences endure.

I shall always smile at the memory,
Share *the day I sang* with future family
My grandchildren will say
My Grandma sang at the opening

Of that beautiful building.
Historic event, outstanding day.

This belongs to the people of Dundee
Art and culture for us all, not the few;
Native and adopted, enriches our lives.
Meh toon, oor museum o Skohtish design,
Fur abudee, wee'r guid uh sharehin!
Proud to be a Dundonian.

Words from Duende Voices, Loadsaweeminsingin',
Lochee Linties and the Noteables

Epilogue

And so we end this anthology, on a note of optimism and hope for the city of Dundee. A hope that the V&A, and associated 'regeneration', can serve the people that call Dundee their home. After all, there have been some troubling developments over the last few months; the reopening of Brassica after closure relating to over £30,000 in unpaid wages, the threat to Reading Rooms (Dundee's countercultural heart) by police and an adjacent luxury hotel offering a slice of 'Shoreditch cool', rising rents and ever-dwindling housing conditions (recently culminating in my own eviction), and the loss of two major employers in the city, Michelin and McGill. What the work in this anthology shows, above all else, is that the people will not be silenced. Dundee has survived worse traumas than gentrification, and it will survive again. The city has a thriving creative community, that is of no doubt – the only problem with the narrative is the idea that this is something completely new. Dundee has always produced outspoken, innovative artists and writers. Some have already been mentioned – Mary Brooksbank, Joseph Lee, even William McGonagall...

McGonagall may not have been the most accomplished writer – but whether or not his work was somewhat satirical is still a hot topic in the city, and it will continue to be so. If McGonagall was in on it or not, he was a sensation in his time and managed to regularly sell out venues. In fact, when he came along, Dundee already had a rich tradition of both radical and popular art that engaged with the community it was born out of.

In the sixteenth century, the Wedderburn brothers created ground-breaking writing across all three genres, while playing an active role locally. All three, but John in particular, masterminded the Gude and Godlie Ballatis – the first publication that encouraged the commons to sing about God in their own language, to the tune of their own beloved songs. The Complaynt of Scotland is often attributed to Robert Wedderburn, and it cradles the line between a radical political tract and an astonishingly powerful work of Middle-Scots prose. The writings of James are sadly lost to us now, but his public plays on John the Baptist and Dionysius the Tyrant proved to be a thorn in the side of the establishment, to the point where he was exiled in France.

In the eighteenth century, McGonagall was nothing but a latecomer to an already thriving Dundee poetry scene. The huge success of The People's Journal, amongst other publications, ensured that Dundee was the centre of a new mass-movement – a moment when, for the first time, working-class writers were able to regularly see their work in print and enjoy wide-scale readership. This encouraged endless innovation, but the work of Poute is especially notable. Writing in a thick East-Coast vernacular dialect, with deliberately bad grammar and phonetic spelling, Poute parodied middle-class assumptions of what the working-classes would write. His work today reads as truly experimental and inaccessible, but it was again, incredibly successful in its time. If you squint through the challenging style – the humour is still as sharp and universal today. James Young Geddes took inspiration from Walt Whitman to create visionary poems in free verse that did not hold back in their political content – targeting subjects from Alyth Council to Glendale, the wealthy Jute-baron. He also used religion to explore the issues of the day – with his collection The New Jerusalem offering a radical view. Jesus returns to Dundee, and the council do not hesitate to crucify him for preaching tolerance and charity to the poor. One poetic persona dies, only to find Heaven populated with bourgeois bureaucrats, he opts for Hell instead. These figures established themselves against a backdrop of poetic engagement in the city, built around the Poet's Box and Literary Societies that met in coffeeshops on the Murraygate.

On to the twentieth century, where Dundee was at the forefront of the century's most contentious debates. In terms of literature, Dundee was heavily neglected by the leading figures of the Scottish Literary Renaissance. Hugh MacDiarmid famously said that 'Dundee is dust', while Grassic Gibbon described the city as a 'frowsy fisher-wife addicted to gin and infanticide'. Casual sexism aside, these comments betray an utter ignorance of cultural life in Dundee. It may well be that chauvinism had something to do with the reluctance of Scotland's literary icons to engage with the city – as Dundee served as a hub of Suffragette activity. Winston Churchill's time as MP in Dundee is not the most well-remembered of his political offices – as he left in disgrace. During one campaign, a woman called Mary Maloney followed him around ringing a large bell – I chose to use this image as the first Amplify poster. He was eventually beaten by Edwin Scrymgeour, the only ever elected representative of the Prohibition Party. In short, Dundee decided that they would rather give up drink than endure another minute of Churchill's leadership.

The city had many problems, and it still does – but even the most elementary dip into the city archives reveals that Dundonians have always taken solace in art and culture. Even in the grip of Thatcher's eighties, Dundee was a hub for neoist activity through the activities of Pete Horobin and his D.A.T.A. initiative. The avant-garde was active through the most challenging of political eras – and actively tried to use experimental art for the social good. The 'Festival of Non-Participation' at Dundee Resource Center for the Unemployed was a key moment in this exchange.

Avant-garde activity in the eighties occurred alongside innovation in the world of Community Theatre – when The Rep and the Dudhope Arts Centre pioneered a series of socially-engaged, locally-focused productions. Witch's Blood events included the whole city and managed to recreate historic Dundee. Those shows paved the way for a 1989 Dundee Mystery Play, which set the New Testament in contemporary Tayside – pitting the son of man against Duncan Herd, a money-hungry and exploitative local councillor.

Dundee's cultural scene today is at a high again, but the risks are apparent in the current situation. The creation of a 'cultural quarter' in the west-end of the city that surrounds the university, has led to the emergence of a bubble. Practitioners and consumers make use of the city for art and culture without ever engaging with the areas outwith the centre and the west-end. I have lived in the city full-time for six-years, and I have attended countless cultural events – and I can count on my hands the amount that have been rooted in social-awareness and finding solutions to the serious issues we face. My dad moved to Charleston when I was a child, and the difference between my experience here growing up, and my experience since I came to university, is stark. This has little to do with the changes that have taken place in Dundee, and it has everything to do with geography. I have known people who have attended university for four years, having never met an actual Dundonian. This is a fundamental problem. As the housing market continues to collapse, and with more students coming to the city with every year, we must seriously consider what will happen if the student community is pushed further out of the city. This will mean more displacement for local people, more homelessness, and more drug abuse. Some self-awareness and personal responsibility is needed in Dundee, especially from those active in the university and the art community.

However, we have seen the examples of London and Glasgow – and countless other cities. If a place is going to take a stand and ensure that the voice of the people is heard, then Dundee can and should be that place. The history of the city tells us that. From the siege by Cromwell, to the horror of the Jute-Mills, and the demolition of beloved monuments in the seventies – Dundee has endured, Dundee has persisted. We now have a beautiful museum, and if all goes according to plan – it will be fundamental to making the city a better place.

Contributors

James Barrowman is a twenty-three year old writer and editor, and this marks his first publication. What he lacks in experience, he makes up for with enthusiasm and plucky zeal. He has been running the Amplify writing group since Summer 2018.

Paul Malgrati lives in Dundee and researches Scottish Literature at St Andrews University. A native of Paris, he writes poetry in Scots, English, and French.

Erin Farley is a researcher, writer and storyteller based in Dundee. She works in Dundee Central Library's Local History Centre, and her PhD thesis was on poetry and song communities in Victorian Dundee. She is one of three co-hosts on The Beans podcast, which tells true stories from many sources.

Andy Jackson was born in 1965 in Salford and moved to Scotland in 1992. In his day job, he is Learning & Teaching Librarian at Dundee University. He edited *Whaleback City* with Bill Herbert, and his most recent collection *A Beginner's Guide To Cheating*, was published in 2016 by Red Squirrel Press.

Anna Stewart is a recipient of a Scottish Book Trust New Writers Award and was shortlisted for The Royal Academy and Pin Drop Short Story Award. Anna's stories have also been published in Riptide Journal, Gutter Magazine, New Writing Dundee and The Weekend Read. Recently, she was invited to read her work in Scots at the Scottish Parliament.

Donald Henry is a narrowly published writer, who attempts to distil the essence of literature from the raw mash of Dundee life. He finds it well-nigh impossible to write about himself in third person.

AR Crow is a poet, performer and trainee psychiatrist. Their publications to date include poems in We Were Always Here: A Queer Words Anthology, published by 404 Ink. They like bookshops, brunch and Bronski Beat. @IAmACr0w

E.G. Smith lives in Dundee and writes poetry as well as prose – with an emphasis on transcribing overheard conversations.

Miguel Alcazár lives in Dundee. He has published one novel, *Bulevar 20* (in Spanish), and his short fiction in English has been published by Gravel Magazine, Chicago Literati, and Maudlin House.

Matt Townsend is a writer from Western Australia who lives in Dundee.

Cheryl McGregor is a third year English literature and creative writing student. In her spare time she can be found capitalising on free wine at exhibitions or at the cinema-house.

Laura Strathern is a graduate of Dundee's MLitt in Creative Writing. She is from Edinburgh. She does not own any beetles.

Reece Robertson is a recent graduate of Dundee University, with focus in the fields of creative writing and comics. Hailing from Whitfield, Dundee himself.

Zan de Parry is a poet from the Midwestern United States. He's been published variously in print and online, most recently Unsaid, Fluland, BathHouse, Tabloid 13 and Gramma, and is author to the chapbook *Vibraphone* (Brest Press).

W.N. Herbert is Dundee's Makar, mostly published by Bloodaxe Books and teacher of Creative Writing at Newcastle University. Recent publications include *Omnesia* and *Murder Bear*, both 2013, with a new book of poems coming out in 2020 (by which time he'll hopefully have come up with the title).

Sue Haigh is studying the MLitt in Creative Writing. She is one of 150 singers who opened the V&A in September. She is currently working with the archives at the Glasgow Women's Library.

Printed in Great Britain
by Amazon